# Beyond Boomerang

**FORMICA**

# Beyond
# Boomerang

## A Celebration of 110 Years
## of Formica® Patterns

Shawn Patrick Tubb

*Dedicated to the generations of Formica Team Members who have helped build the Formica Brand for the past 110 years*

## CREDITS

**Historian and Researcher**
Renee Hytry Derrington, Formica Corporation

**Editor and Art Direction**
Meghan Howell, Formica Corporation

**Copy Editor**
Amy Gath, Formica Corporation
Renee Hytry Derrington, Formica Corporation

**Project Contributors**
Amy Gath, Renee Hytry Derrington, Meghan Howell, Gerri Chmiel, Bob Ford, Darla McCollister Ford, Sharon de Leon, Dianna Marra, Kathleen Streitenberger, Tracy Shannon, Cincinnati Museum Center Archives and Manuscripts Department

**Design**
Mayfly Design, Minneapolis, MN

**Color and Retouching**
Artwork prepared for printing by color specialist Timothy Meegan

## LEGAL

Published by Formica Corporation, Cincinnati, Ohio

ISBN: 979-8-218-16206-1

A Cataloging-in-Publication record for this book is available from the Library of Congress.

Front cover background image: Aeriel Fields, the Laurinda Spear Collection

First Printing: 2023
Printed in Canada

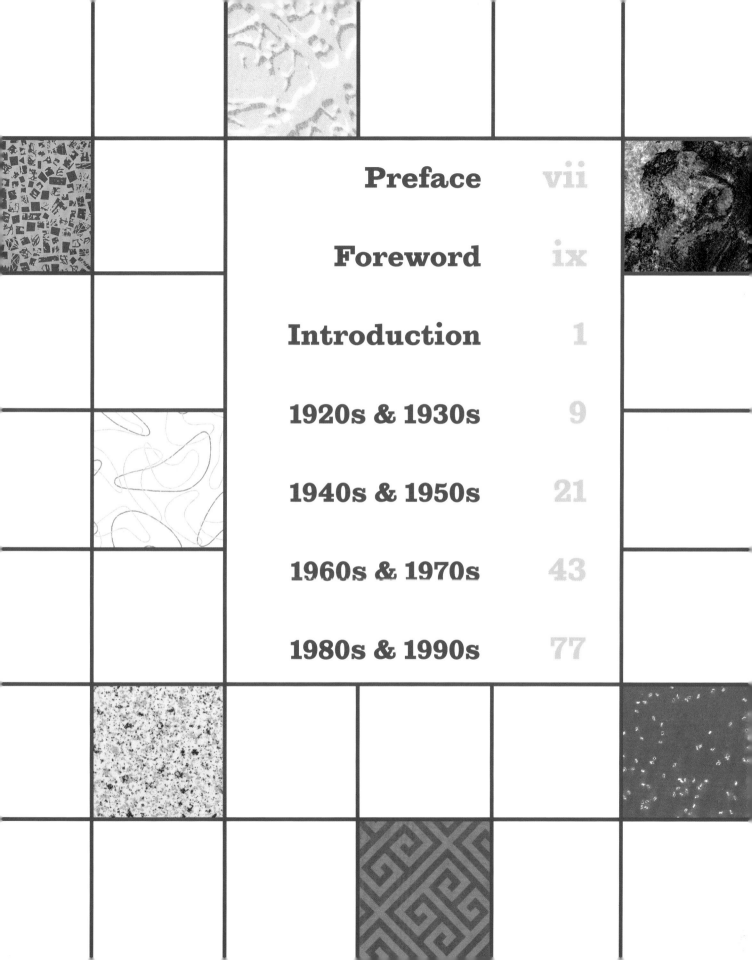

**Preface** vii

**Foreword** ix

**Introduction** 1

**1920s & 1930s** 9

**1940s & 1950s** 21

**1960s & 1970s** 43

**1980s & 1990s** 77

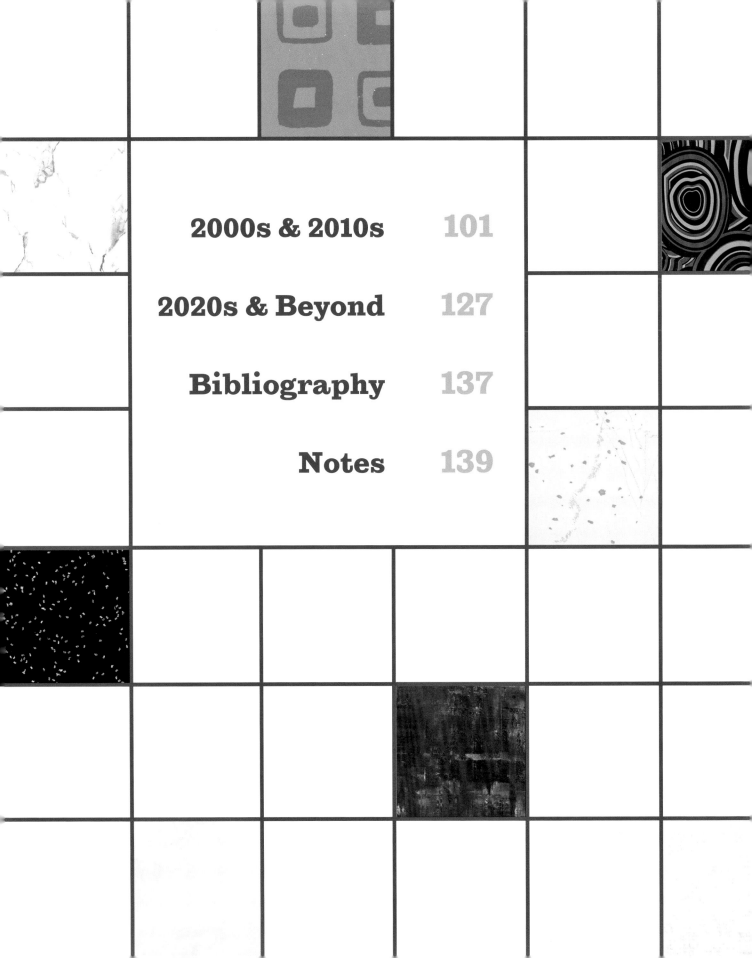

2000s & 2010s    101

2020s & Beyond    127

Bibliography    137

Notes    139

# PREFACE

As the inventor of the category, the Formica® Brand brought to the market a difficult-to-imitate combination of beautiful and flexible aesthetics and incredible functionality — all at a highly affordable price. Even as other material options emerged and were embraced by residential and commercial customers over the last century, the ability of the Formica Brand to deliver on its triangle of benefits has helped it remain a surfacing leader and a global design staple.

As such, it was with great enthusiasm that Broadview acquired Formica Corporation in 2019, bringing the Formica Brand into a family of global surfacing leaders that includes the FENIX®, Arpa and TRESPA® brands, and opening the doors to Broadview's large network of technology, design and sustainability resources to help power the future. Even though laminate's product technology has been largely unchanged since its invention, our products have a remarkably favorable environmental footprint based on the fact that they are predominantly wood-based combined with great durability. As we look to the future, we are working hard to minimize any remaining impact by further increasing the bio-based content of our products.

With this book, we celebrate the 110th anniversary of the Formica Brand and explore its proud design history, showcasing some of the most iconic patterns and the people and stories behind them. Whether it was the natural world, modern art or popular culture, the Formica Brand Designers drew inspiration from a variety of sources that helped the brand not only reflect the evolving world, but also influence the national (and global) conversation.

This book, however, is more than just a celebration of Formica Brand's patterns. It also is a tribute to the power of creativity and innovation, as well as to the work of generations of Formica Brand associates who have designed, produced, marketed, sold and moved Formica Laminate around the world so well.

The future of the Formica Brand is exciting. Grounded in the triangle of benefits delivered at its invention and paired with the global strength and leadership of the Broadview family, I have great confidence in the future ahead. Onward to the next 110 years!

Matthijs Schoten
CEO, Broadview Holding

Glass Cloth, 2022

# FOREWORD

**W**hile headlines and advertising declared plastic as the wonder-material of the 20th-century, Formica was waging a quieter, stealthier campaign that spread across surfaces in homes, offices, factories, schools, restaurants, and hotels. With incredible speed and geographic reach, Formica gained its foothold among glass, metal, wood, and tile, materials with nearly ancient pedigrees. Part of what made its adoption so swift was its readiness to be a good-humored partner to traditional materials, a hard-working friend that could be applied to any substrate, that looked good against the increasingly non-porous surfaces of modern kitchens and bathrooms. The revolution of Formica heralded a new tactility for modern life, one that could sustain the everyday indignities of spills, cigarettes, cleaning agents, and hard-wearing use. It coincided with the escalating awareness and demand for new standards of hygiene and cleanliness.

But it would be wrong to focus on the extroverted pragmatism of Formica. It has become such a landmark for design and materials not just as a workhorse, but also because of its still-magical alchemy of paper, color, and pattern. Try to imagine the 20th-century without Formica. It is center-stage in our diners, bowling alleys, boats, doctors offices, laundromats, classrooms, supermarkets, and the countless examples of furniture that found freedom in its eager-to-please finish.

There is a parallelism between Formica and the rise of modern packaging: both are products of increasingly sophisticated industrial paper and printing processes. Both marshalled the allure of color and modern design to everyday life. Many of the same designers who redesigned America's supermarkets, stores, kitchens and dining rooms also used Formica or were hired to develop its patterns: Morris B. Sanders, Jr., Donald Deskey, Raymond Loewy, Henry Dreyfus, Walter Dorwin Teague, Brooks Stevens, and Charles and Ray Eames. As a tastemaker, Formica has always honored its heritage. Because of its deep identification with mid-century modernism, Formica will always have a "retro" soul. It has a boomerang-shaped heart. But successive waves of new patterns, textures and colors have anticipated and kept pace with the enduring appeal of this magical, hardworking friend.

Abbott Miller, Pentagram

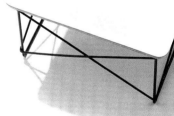

Abbott Miller designed Formica® Anniversary Collection featured on Eames Wire Base Low Tables

Endless Graytone, 2013

# INTRODUCTION

**I**n a world where brands emerge and then disappear as quickly as one can snap their fingers, Formica Brand's 110th Anniversary represents a unique accomplishment. Through meaningful global change, the brand has evolved, persisted and prospered. A significant contributor to the brand's longevity has been its iconic patterns. Since the early 20th century, the designers of Formica decorative laminates have used the language of pattern to create enduring designs that have been employed in homes, hotels, offices, schools and restaurants the world over. The Formica Brand's distinctive and highly adaptable visual language has influenced the global design conversation, while at the same time being shaped by world events and the advent of new technologies. This year, as we celebrate Formica Brand's 110th anniversary, we also celebrate more than a century of bold patterns and the talented designers who developed them.

While the underlying component layers have changed little since its inception, the magic of Formica laminate lies in its seemingly infinite regeneration over the years to match the current moment. As one surveys the depths of the company's historic catalog, it becomes clear that through the use of pattern, texture, and color, the character of each progressive collection went to great effort to echo our collective values, illuminate the promise (and limitations) of current technology, and perhaps even offer a glimpse of our aspirations in a given moment in time. This is accomplished not simply through the pattern on paper but through awareness of and contribution to the larger dialogue.

Some of the preeminent designers of the 20th century have played a key role in keeping the Formica brand at the forefront of that conversation, among them Morris B. Sanders, Brooks Stevens, Raymond Loewy, Laurinda Spear, Abbott Miller, and Jonathan Adler. The company also employed a cadre of talented artisans that composed and executed a significant majority of the Formica library as well as the technological innovations that helped bring those designs to market. These included Jack Cochrane, Lorraine Elton, Bob Ford, J. Allen Montei, Sharon de Leon, Alessandro De Gregori, and Renee Hytry Derrington, just to name a few.

# ORIGIN STORY

Formica Corporation originated during a period of rapid societal and technological change in the United States, and so the company's history closely intertwined with that of the country throughout the 20th century. The turn of the 19th to 20th centuries marked a shift into the modern age — driven by technology, communication, and the interconnectedness of a new global society. In 1913, the same year that Formica was founded, Henry Ford revolutionized manufacturing with the first assembly line plant and New York's Armory Show introduced Americans to a dazzling new world of modern art with exhibitions by dozens of European artists — Cassatt, Duchamp, Monet, van Gogh, and Picasso — on display for the first time in North America. The following year, the Panama Canal opened and the first World War began - examples of the seismic shift toward globalism.

Technology and industry were changing the way people experienced design and the environments in which they lived; the world was getting smaller and seemed to be spinning on its axis at a much faster clip. Thus was born the reactionary Arts and Crafts movement of the late 19th century, which sought to maintain the human connection to the process of making during an era of

"A retrospective glance at interior design in this century indicates rapidly shifting popular preferences. The ever-evolving array of colors and patterns pressed and preserved in Formica brand laminate is a particularly appropriate barometer of stylistic change because Formica laminate is certainly one of the quintessential interior design materials of this century. A plastic building material that has revolutionized the interior landscapes of our homes, commercial establishments, and institutions, it has also reflected the transformation and recurrence of colors and patterns in time. And colors and patterns, as we will see, correspond to societal moods and movements and provide an additional dimension to the history of popular culture."[1]

— Marybeth Shaw

industrial mechanization and an idealized return to historic motifs and traditional methods. Meanwhile, the Art Nouveau movements looked to nature for inspiration in decoration and form, while leaning into the possibilities afforded by new technologies and materials such as cast iron, aluminum, and glass.

At the beginning of the 20th century, rapid developments in technology and science opened new possibilities in materials and gave rise to Art Deco, a style that continued to utilize new technology but included an eclectic mix of historical references and machine-age symbolism. A more strict interpretation of Modernism developed in parallel that desired a clean break with history and decoration, focusing on an idealized vision of design that would operate like a machine. While Art Nouveau and Art Deco were originally reserved for the upper classes, the Arts and Crafts and Modernism of this period sought to make good design and functional materials available to everyone.

Formica decorative laminate was born against this backdrop of transitional tension and succeeded in marrying these seemingly opposite ideals. Through a blend of human ingenuity and handcraft came a highly durable and aesthetic material that allowed businesses and homeowners alike an opportunity to enjoy high-end finishes at an accessible price.

Founded in 1913 by Herbert A. Faber and Daniel J. O'Conor, the Formica Insulation Company was a start-up focused on using new techniques in plastic laminate for industrial and electrical applications. The young engineers met in 1907 while working for Westinghouse in Pittsburgh, immediately after college. A shared entrepreneurial spirit drove Faber and O'Conor to leave their jobs and begin their own joint venture in Cincinnati in 1913. The firm focused on producing high-quality insulating products for their clients and by 1914, they had already begun manufacturing flat sheet laminate that could be incorporated into other manufacturers' products or applied to surfaces. Soon the company had diversified its clients beyond electrical insulation to include mechanical applications such as parts for aviation and textiles, as well as electronic uses in radios on commercial shipping and naval vessels. As the decade came to a close, Formica Insulation Company's annual sales had reached $175,000 and their future was bright.[2]

By the following decade, the Formica company would revolutionize plastics with the creation of decorative sheet laminate — the foundation for a library that would eventually grow into hundreds of unique patterns and colors. As was

Herbert A. Faber

Daniel J. O'Conor

Factory and office buildings at the Spring Grove
Avenue location. From Formica: Forty Years of
Steady Vision, 1953

First rented plant, Second and Main
Streets, Cincinnati, Ohio

Walton, Ky. March 17, 1913

Herbert Faber and D. J. O'Conor of Pittsburgh, Pa. desiring to
start a manufactory in Cincinnati, Ohio for electrical insulating under
some name to be hereafter selected and to be hereafter incorporated; and
desiring to raise $7500.00 cash capital to begin said business; Now, it
is agreed between said Faber and O'Conor on one side and J. G. Tomlin
on the other that said Tomlin will furnish said ($7500.00) Seventy-Five
hundred dollars on the following terms and conditions, namely:—Said
Tomlin will take a one-third interest in said business and furnish
Twenty-Five hundred ($2500.00) dollars of same and said Tomlin will lend
said Faber and O'Conor Twenty-Five hundred ($2500.00) dollars each at
seven percent (7%) or so much thereof as they need, each of them to
endorse for the other.

Said Faber and O'Conor being experienced men in electrical work
are beginning May 1st, to give their whole time and attention to this
work for one hundred and fifty ($150.00) dollars per month for six months,
and after that they are to have One hundred and seventy-five ($175.00)
dollars per month provided the business is on basis to justify it.
Said Tomlin is not to have any salary unless future wants in the way
of financial or legal services make it proper; but to cover actual
expenses in an advisory and consulting way, said Tomlin shall be allowed
One Hundred ($100.00) dollars for first term of six months.

4

Early application of Formica® laminate
and 1913 letter from Formica: Forty Years
of Steady Vision, 1953

1927 Sales meeting, from Formica:
Forty Years of Steady Vision, 1953

1920s Cutting machine, located in Spring Grove plant.
From Formica: Forty Years of Steady Vision, 1953

Early manufacturing of Formica® Laminate moved from a rented plant on Second and Main Streets in 1913, to a rented plant in 1914 on Spring Grove Avenue and Alabama Streets and then to a purchased plant in 1919 on Spring Grove Avenue and Winton Road in Cincinnati.

suggested by its original tagline, '*Beauty Bonded Formica*' decorative laminates represent a marriage of art and technology. The creative energy expended by the company's technicians, designers, and artists in pattern development and quality assurance is well-matched by the time and effort invested by its many factory workers, scientists, and engineers in creating the advanced and durable materials that brought these works of art to life.

# HOW DECORATIVE LAMINATE IS MADE

The pattern is etched into a metal cylinder so that large sheets of paper can be printed continuously as they roll through in a type of rotary printing process called rotogravure. The printed sheet, or décor paper, is then saturated with melamine resin and pulled through an oven to cure. Sheets of kraft paper are impregnated with another type of resin, cured, and stacked together to form the core. The décor paper is placed on top of the core, a protective overlay is placed on the decorative layer, and the stack is machine-pressed using engraved steel plates to add texture (or smooth plates for a glossy finish) to the laminate as it cures for about 60 minutes under high heat (300°F) and extreme pressure (1,400 psi). Once this process is complete, the result is a highly durable and attractive sheet of laminate that can be attached to a substrate to create furniture, countertops, millwork, and more.

HOW DECORATIVE LAMINATE IS MADE GRAPHIC FROM FORMICA FOREVER, 2013

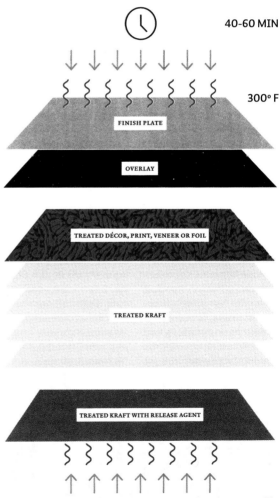

40-60 MIN

300° F

FINISH PLATE

OVERLAY

TREATED DÉCOR, PRINT, VENEER OR FOIL

TREATED KRAFT

TREATED KRAFT WITH RELEASE AGENT

# CHAPTER ONE

# 1920s & 1930s

**T**he 1920s were years of explosive growth and prosperity for many Americans following the economic difficulties of World War I. Despite the specter of Prohibition beginning in 1919, the Jazz Age of the 20s was a period of expanding worldviews and shifting social norms. Marked progress in women's rights was finally realized, starting with the right to vote in 1920, opportunities outside the home, and a relative degree of sartorial liberation. Film and broadcasting advanced to include "talkies" and radio stations throughout the country. In 1925 the Bauhaus changed its focus to what would become the International Style and the "International Exhibition of Modern Decorative and Industrial Arts" in

Paris led to the popularization of Art Deco. The decade was most closely associated with luxury and glamour in design and materials and colors such as dark woods, silver, gold, and vibrant colors like teal, maroon, and goldenrod.

The 1930s stood in stark contrast to the glittery optimism of the previous decade, being largely defined by economic struggle and the landmark government programs meant to combat those downward pressures. The stock market crash of 1929 and the beginning of a severe economic downturn were followed by the New Deal and Works Progress Administration (WPA) which invested heavily in public infrastructure and the arts. Though the Great Depression ended the carefree decadence of the Roaring Twenties, commercial enterprises like cinemas and department stores still attempted to evoke wealth and provide escapism with their materials and aesthetics. The film industry debuted movies like *The Wizard of Oz* and *Gone with the Wind* to help distract Americans from the realities of high unemployment and food shortages. Art Deco reached its peak in the early 1930s and evolved into Art Moderne or Streamline Style during the latter half of the decade. This new style was more future-focused, celebrating the machine age, and brought an increase in chrome finishes with colors that became more subdued hues of blues, greens, and reds, with white stucco as a frequent backdrop.

# INVENTION AND GROWTH

The earliest products made by the Formica Insulation Company were utilitarian, often hidden inside engines or used in machinery and electronics where the aesthetics were of little concern. By the early 1920s however, Faber and O'Conor saw an opportunity to capitalize on the prosperity of the day and bring their sheet laminate to consumer products and architectural installations. Its durability and material properties made it an ideal solution for cladding popular new devices and starting in 1921, Formica® laminates in solid black and brown first found their way into American homes as part of the wildly popular do-it-yourself home radio kits. These subdued colors were not intentional, but rather the dark tints that were standard for plastics at the time, as the resins in use were inherently brown and amber-colored.

During a period of intensive growth for their company, Faber and O'Conor expanded the workforce with strategic hires and pushed to develop new products. Sales in 1920 were around $400,000 and had jumped to $1,900,000 in 1923 and then were over $3,000,000 just a year later. The company's chemist Clarence M. Hargrave filed a patent in 1923 for a process using a printed sheet as the decorative surface for laminate, opening the door to new possibilities in pattern and color. The following year, the Formica Insulation Co. hired John (Jack) D. Cochrane, Jr. as its first Director of Research to focus on both decorative and industrial applications, and in 1925, hired its first Director of Engineering, George H. Clark, to help grow the operations and increase efficiency. The company's scientists and technicians then developed methods to print multi-colored designs on the decór paper and to use rotogravure cylinders for continuous printing. These innovations were critical at a time when Bakelite's basic patents were expiring and many companies were trying to get into the decorative laminate business.[3]

# EARLY PATTERN EXPERIMENTS

Evidence of early experimentation in pattern development during the pre-war period includes designs with various effects, primarily in ruddy or amber colors, over a dark background. Described as "organic and crazed patterns," they ranged from ethereal marbled looks and early wood grains to abstract cellular structures and a graphic wallpaper appearance. Very few early samples remain, but those that do illustrate a desire to create a diversity of patterns and push the limits of the technology available at the time.[4]

Between 1924 and 1926, the Formica brand introduced the world's first patterns on decorative laminate. Cochrane had developed a faux, dark wood grain — selected to complement the solid black and brown laminate being used on radios at the time. The team also created a green marble pattern intended to replace the metal

Early applications of Formica® laminate were industrial.

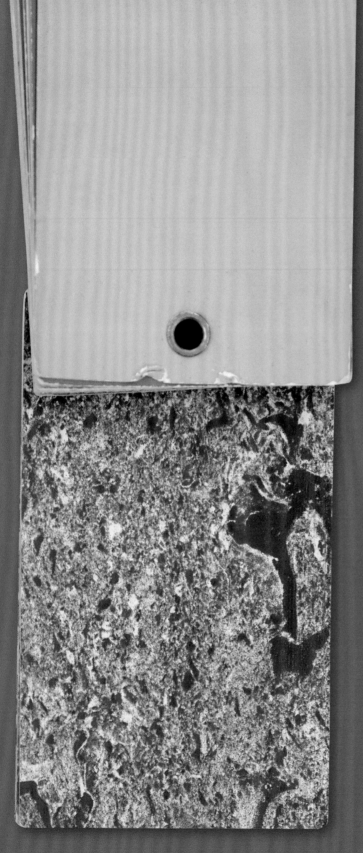
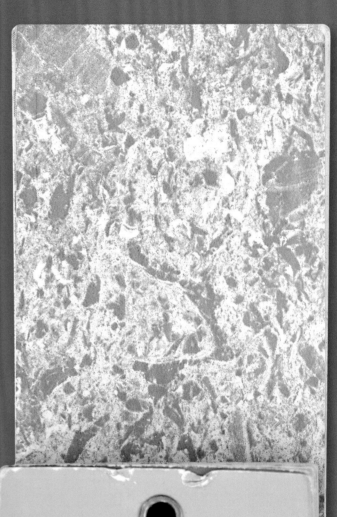

Beauty Bonded

**FORMICA**

Reg. U.S. Pat. Off.

57-MR-1

GREEN MARBLE

Marble 1927

Early engineers work in product development in the research lab at the Winton Place Plant

strips on soda fountain equipment. The Liquid Carbonic Corporation initiated the request, which involved photographing a tile of dark green marble and using the resulting images to create a printing plate.

In July of 1927, the Formica Co. was granted two U.S. patents for having created the first faux, light wood grain laminate, which employed the use of an opaque sheet under the décor paper to prevent the dark brown resin in the underlying layers from showing through. This would later allow Formica to expand into more uses on furniture and millwork with a wider variety of wood colors. However, these early patterns were still too crude for furniture or high-end interiors, so black remained the most common sheet sold.

In 1931, they took another big step forward in the commercial sector with the advent of cigarette-proof laminates, integrating a thin layer of aluminum between the décor layer and kraft paper layers below. This led to an explosion of installations on countertops, tables, walls, and other surfaces primarily in public venues — diners, soda fountains, train cars, bus stations, and ocean liners. Because plastic laminates were such a novel material in the 1930s and due to the popularity of glossy black paired with chrome as part of the Art Deco aesthetic, Formica laminate was considered an avant-garde and glamorous material. Well-known designers such as Paul Frankl, Gilbert Rohde, Morris B. Sanders,

Formica Realwood advertisement, 1946

and Donald Deskey were using laminates for the interiors and custom furniture of some of New York's wealthiest clientele. High-profile installations during this period included Radio City Music Hall in New York City, the Library of Congress and Treasury Building in Washington DC, Harrods Department Store in London, and the luxury ocean liner RMS Queen Mary. Sales dropped by more than 50% during the Great Depression but fortunately, movie theaters, newsstands, and institutions were still building.[5]

The Hurlbut Paper Company in South Lee, Massachusetts began supplying solid color specialty paper that could be saturated with resins in 1936, allowing the Formica Company to produce solid color laminate (other than black and brown) for the first time. However, technical limitations during that period meant that the solid color laminates were recommended only for vertical installations. In 1937, the company announced *Realwood* which used genuine wood veneer treated with melamine as the decór layer. Developed in-house by Jack Cochrane and George Clark, *Realwood* introduced Formica laminate into furniture and interiors that demanded a more realistic look. Another advance that year was the replacement of thio-resins with melamine resin which had superior durability and aesthetics allowing Formica laminate to be used on high-use areas like kitchen and diner table tops.

An early paper sample set showing the Linen pattern
on top of Gray Pearl, 1949

The company greatly expanded its marketing to architects and designers in late 1937 and 1938, releasing a range of over 70 colors and patterns that were published in trade catalogs. These included the opalescent *Decorated*, an early version of *Pearl*, and the Series H which was a textile pattern similar to *Linen*. The solid colors were available in two grades: the Series B was made with more stable resins and could be produced in light shades, while the Series A was the more budget-conscious, standard option. Series A included two unique patterns with black backgrounds and a marbled paper effect in yellow for *Black and Gold* and in green for *Verde Antique*. In addition, several faux wood grain patterns were added alongside the authentic veneers of the *Realwood* line.

As the decade ended, the 1939 New York World's Fair promised to move Americans past the realities of the Great Depression and show its 44 million visitors what the future could hold. The expo's theme was "The World of Tomorrow" and General Motors' *Futurama* exhibit, designed by Norman Bel Geddes, foretold the auto-oriented cities of the post-war era. Meanwhile, General Electric's pavilion showcased the marvels of modern living including televisions and all-electric appliances like a refrigerator, dishwasher, and vacuum cleaner - all designed to make the homemaker's life easier and more efficient, something Formica laminate would soon do.

"*The designers working on a pattern project must have knowledge of historic influences in fine arts, architecture, and decorative motifs of peoples and nations through history. They must have day to day work experience on products in major classifications such as home furnishings, housewares, building materials, as well as design of large scale commercial structures. Equally important is first hand study and familiarity through comparative shopping of decorative materials with particular attention to laminates. Finally, they must be aware of the 'pattern' of Formica sales and special company marketing knowledge of the industry. It is through this cross-breeding of research, experience and current trends that pattern design decisions are made.*"[6]

— Jack Alexander

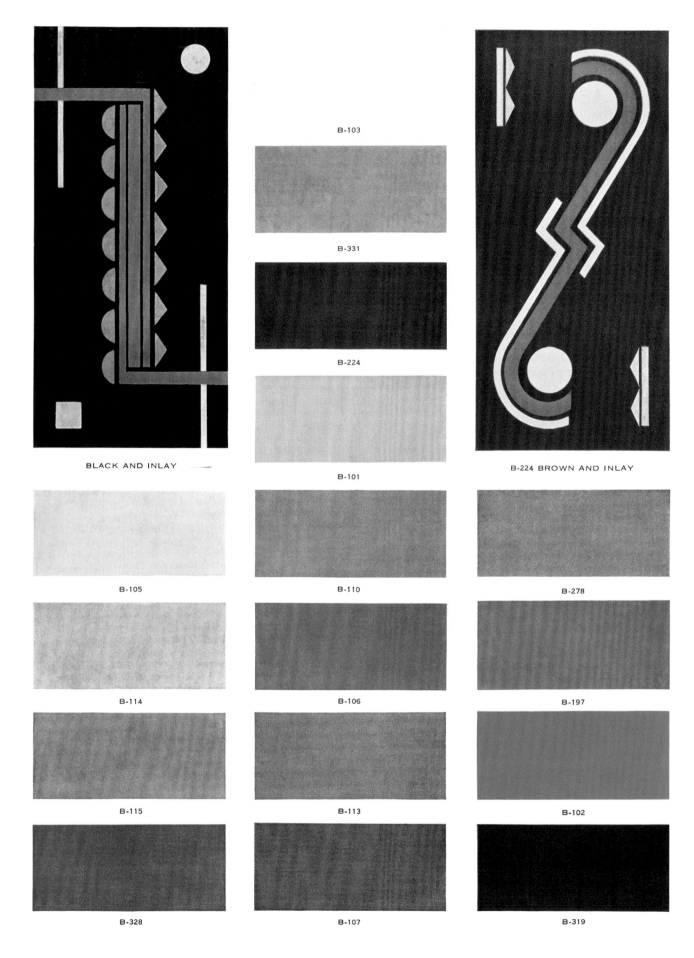

BLACK AND INLAY

B-224 BROWN AND INLAY

B-103

B-331

B-224

B-101

B-105

B-110

B-278

B-114

B-106

B-197

B-115

B-113

B-102

B-328

B-107

B-319

No. 24 DECORATED—B

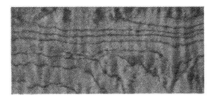

LIGHT MAPLE—B

LIGHT WALNUT—B

VERDE ANTIQUE—B

No. 25 DECORATED—B

STUMP WALNUT

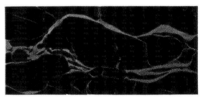

BLACK AND GOLD—B

B-108

B-35

BROWN MARBLE—B

B-116

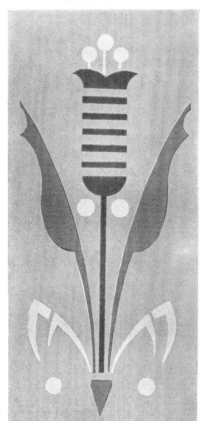

B-114 AND INLAY

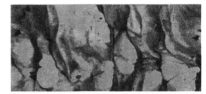

No. 10 DECORATED

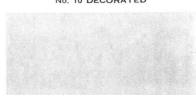

B-282

B-386

Formica Insulation Company
brochure, 1940

B-32

# CHAPTER TWO

# 1940s & 1950s

**T**he 1940s were dominated by the Second World War which had started just a few months after the 1939 World's Fair had begun. By the U.S. entry into the war in 1941, the country's creative energy and industrial focus shifted to the war effort. The end of hostilities in 1945 ushered in a huge wave of unprecedented growth and an accompanying air of optimism, while the imprint of wartime efforts continued to change the daily lives of all civilians in ways large and small. Inventions that were originally intended for military applications made their way into civilian life by the mid-century period, including the first computers, the microwave oven, and the jet engine. Anxiety and fascination with the atomic bomb led to an infatuation with outer space and all things extraterrestrial in popular culture.

The "Baby Boom" was accompanied by rapid suburbanization as public and private investment subsidized a glut of new housing for the returning GIs and their growing families. 1940s swing music gave way to the energetic rock 'n' roll tunes of the 1950s. Television saw mainstream adoption during the postwar period, with the majority of American homes owning a TV by the end of the 1950s. Taken together, these paint a picture of cheery optimism, widespread prosperity, and the rise of a sizable middle class. It's no wonder then that the patriotic red, white, and blue along with the austere colors of the war years were overshadowed by brighter pastels in pink, turquoise, and chartreuse by the late 1940s and 1950s. These colors began showing up not just in clothing and advertisements, but even in automobiles and durable goods like kitchen appliances.

# POST-WAR GROWTH

With the United States entering World War II, the Formica Insulation Company's production of commercial products came to a halt and was replaced by new items created for military applications including propellers and many other parts for airplanes. The need for wartime materials was so great that the company's sales nearly quadrupled between 1940 and 1943. Meanwhile, management invested in research and marketing to be ready for the post-war economy. The late 1940s and 1950s saw a large investment in modernizing equipment; building a state-of-the-art manufacturing facility, designed especially for the decorative laminate lines; and significantly increasing advertising and sales efforts. The company also began collaborations with outside designers in the late 1940s and this trend continued through the following decade.

The infusion of capital and relationship-building quickly paid off and led to dozens of new patterns being created, a resurgence of commercial and industrial clients, and Formica® laminate entering the booming residential market—especially through kitchen and bathroom countertops and furniture. Of the six million homes built between 1945 and 1953, at least two million had Formica brand surfaces in their kitchens. Before WWII, the company's sales of decorative laminate were roughly 25% of the company's earnings. By 1950, decorative laminate sales were up to 75% of total earnings. The company dropped the word insulation from its name to reflect this shift and became The Formica Company in 1948. On June 28, 1950, the company broke ground in the Cincinnati suburb of Evendale for a state-of-the-art, million-square-foot plant intended strictly for decorative laminate production. [7]

# TERRACE PLAZA HOTEL

Formica laminate was used extensively in the first large hotel project completed in the U.S. after WWII. Started in 1946 and completed in 1948, the 20-story Terrace Plaza Hotel in Cincinnati was a 338-room hotel above two department stores. The first major commercial project for the architecture firm Skidmore, Owings & Merrill (and for their lead designer Natalie de Blois), the International Style design was considered radical at the time and the hotel was widely-published and posited as the future of hospitality and retail. Formica *Realwood* was used prominently to clad the interior of the elevators, the wave-like reception desk,

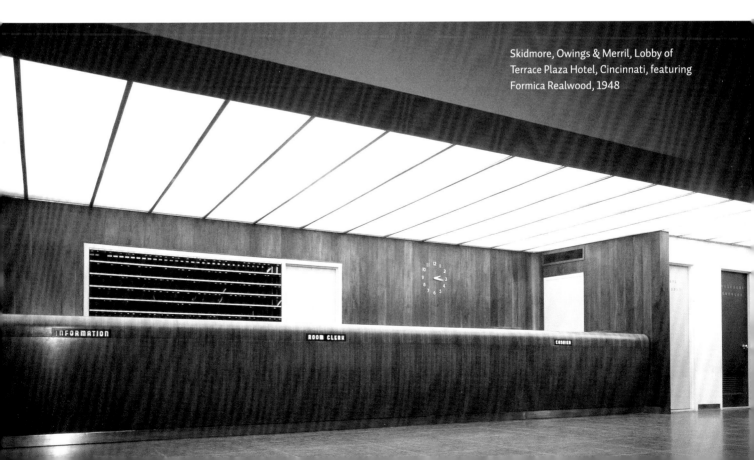

Skidmore, Owings & Merril, Lobby of Terrace Plaza Hotel, Cincinnati, featuring Formica Realwood, 1948

# Whether You Wet Your Whistle At The Bar
## Or Write A Letter Home To Mother . . .

**Beauty Bonded**
# FORMICA
Reg. U. S. Pat. Off.

*at Home with People*
*at Work in Industry*

## *in Cincinnatis Terrace Plaza*

Design: **Skidmore, Owings & Merrill,** architects
Backus Brothers Co., furniture consultants

Every non-upholstered horizontal surface in the 350 guest rooms is cigarette-proof Formica. Note the window seat and "Realwood" shelf behind the day bed.

One of the newest and most startling uses of Formica is in these colorful wash-stand dressing table combinations. Architects are asking for more information. Pictorial literature is now in preparation. We invite your inquiry for "Beauty Bonded Formica for Bathrooms."

Cincinnati Terrace Plaza Advertisement for Formica, 1948.
Image from National Museum of America History Archives
Center, Formica Materials

Your Formica sightseeing tour through Cincinnati's New Terrance Plaza Hotel brochure, 1950-1959

and the walls of the 8th-floor hotel lobby. As advertisements noted at the time, "every non-upholstered horizontal surface in the guest rooms is cigarette-proof Formica" and it was also used extensively in the various restaurants and bars within the building. Each guest room had custom, bentwood furniture by Knoll with black Formica laminate tops and featured built-ins covered in *Realwood*, including a sofa that would slide out from the wall at the push of a button to convert to a bed at night. The bathrooms included innovative curving countertops combining the wash basin and dressing table, topped in a precursor to *Linen*. And acting as a privacy screen near the hotel room door, there was a versatile piece designed to act as a luggage rack, desk, and bar cart — all clad in colorful Formica decorative laminate.[8]

**Beauty Bonded**

FORMICA

Reg. U.S. Pat. Off.

*at Home with People*
*at Work in Industry*

# MORRIS B. SANDERS

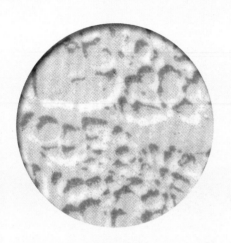

The first pattern known to be designed for the company by an outside consultant and the first Formica laminate pattern to receive a U.S. patent, *Moonglo* was created by the architect Morris B. Sanders in 1948. *Moonglo* was a pattern inspired by the shimmer of moonlight over the surface of a lake. A prominent designer in New York at the time, Sanders was known for designing one of the city's first International Style buildings in 1935 and the Distilled Spirits, Inc. pavilion at the 1939 World's Fair. An early adopter of Formica laminate, Sanders used it throughout his personal residence and studio on the Upper East Side (the aforementioned International Style townhouse). His home, now listed as a New York City Landmark, featured Formica laminate on doors, built-ins, furniture, and more. It won second place in the U.S.A. Plastics Contest, sponsored by Modern Plastics journal in 1936. In addition to architecture, Sanders designed many interiors, ceramics, lighting, consumer products, and one of the first

BBeauty Bonded

FORMICA
Reg. U.S. Pat. Off.
150 - M - 50

YELLO MOONGLO

De. Pat. 157. 683

modular furniture systems. Created for the Mengel furniture company in 1946, the Mengel MODULE was featured in an exhibit at the Museum of Modern Art.[9]

Describing his outlook on the future of decorative products for the Formica Company, vice president J. Roger White said, "we have found an inexhaustible source of distinctive designs for the future - one that can readily yield patterns of almost any character or quality that may be required." Although Sanders said he had dozens more creative ideas like *Moonglo* ready to become patterns, he died unexpectedly later that year, sadly cutting short his participation in the company's creative endeavors.[10]

In addition to a revival of the company's commercial sales, Formica decorative laminate was quickly gaining traction in the residential market as the postwar building boom and rapid suburbanization created many opportunities. The modernization of the American home, in particular of the kitchen, called for the optimization of efficiency, hygiene, and convenience — ideals for which Formica laminate was uniquely suited. Mary and Russel Wright's *Guide to Easier Living*, published in 1950, was an important handbook for homeowners wanting to modernize. The Wrights extolled the virtues of Formica laminate for its durability and ease of cleaning, giving it "Excellent" ratings for use on both horizontal and vertical surfaces. In the early 1950s, the company was spending about $500,000 per year (roughly $5.6 million in today's dollars) on advertising aimed directly at consumers.

In 1949, the Formica Company introduced The Color Range — the first of what would become many named collections of patterns and colors over the years. The range included six "upbeat, blatantly synthetic" patterns "with a whimsical bent." Two existing patterns were rebranded for inclusion: *Linen*, a gridded fabric style, and *Pearl*, based on *Decorated*. New patterns included the organic striations of *Arabesque* and a fabric-inspired design called *Batik*, as well as ten solid colors. Both *Realwood* and the faux wood grain lines were expanded.[11]

Pearl series printed decor paper, date unknown

An early paper sample set the Pearl series, 1949

Arabesque, 1948

LIGHT AQUA

FROST GREEN

CAMELLIA

AZURE

PUTTY GRAY

FLAME

PUMPKIN

PRIMROSE

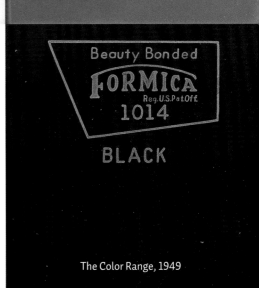

BLACK

The Color Range, 1949

Formica Luxwood
Ad, date unknown.
Image from National
Museum of America
History Archives
Center, Formica
Materials

# BROOKS STEVENS
# DESIGN ASSOCIATES

Another consultant, the industrial design firm Brooks Stevens Associates, was hired in 1949 to develop new patterns for the company. Clifford Brooks Stevens and his company built their reputation through groundbreaking work for nearly 600 clients. Iconic designs such as the prototypical clothes dryer with a glass door, the classic Harley-Davidson motorcycle, the Oscar Mayer Wienermobile, and the Hiawatha train Skytop Lounges (in which Formica *Realwood* was featured prominently) are just a few examples of the firm's work.[12]

Brooks Stevens Design Associates worked with the Formica Company to release several patterns at the beginning of the 1950s. Patterns introduced in 1950 included *Luxwood,* a faux wood grain more realistic than previous versions because it used photographs of real wood, and *Softglo,* a monochromatic variation of *Arabesque* that appeared like a solid color at a distance. In 1951, Formica brand laminate introduced *Skylark* which would become one of the company's most iconic patterns. According to Brooks Stevens, a designer at his company named John Hughes initially penned the design as part of a collection of Formica laminates for use on trains. Its exuberant overlapping kidney shapes captured the energy of Space Age optimism and the Googie style. Also released was *Fernglo* with its graphic leafy fronds, and at the same time, *Softglo* and *Luxwood* were rebranded as *Surfglo* and *Picwood,* with several new colorways introduced for each. Stevens filed a patent application on December 31, 1952 for a pattern assigned to The Formica Company. Called *Homespun,* the design was marketed directly to furniture manufacturers in industry publications such as Furniture Age, National Furniture Review, and Upholstering with a full-page ad by Perry-Brown, Inc.

Softglo series, 1950

Brooks Stevens patterns Skylark, Fernglo, 1951, and Homespun, 1952

# RAYMOND LOEWY ASSOCIATES

The Formica Company began a collaboration with the renowned industrial design firm Raymond Loewy Associates in 1953. Raymond Loewy is considered one of the most influential designers of the 20th century, having created the Streamlined style for trains, buses, and cars; iconic logos for companies including TWA, Shell, and Nabisco; and hundreds of consumer products and appliances. In 1954, Loewy's company designed two new patterns: the "close mottled" stone look of *Italian Marble* and *Capri*, which evoked mosaic tile with its interlocking geometric forms. Building upon the successes of Formica® laminate's sales for use in homes and public spaces, the company released a collection of patterns and vibrant colors in 1954 called The Sunrise Color Line . Styled by Raymond Loewy Associates, the collection included 65 colors — many of them new to the Formica brand. The line was expanded in 1956 to include several recolors of *Linen*, *Pearl*, *and Skylark* along with a new pattern called *Milano*. *Milano*, another variation on marble, was created with a new process called "kaleidoscopic" which resulted in a laminate where no two pieces were identical.

*"Sometimes a pattern may be popular and have a good sales potential, but for one reason or another it is not moving as expected. The fault often lies with choice of color. When a pattern's colors are changed or improved, sales are likely to improve. The history of Formica's Nassau pattern is a good case in point. Four of the six colors in which this pattern was produced in early 1958 were not accepted as well as the other two. One of these four was dropped from the line and the other three were printed in new muted colors — pastels that were just beginning to find favor with the public. The trend of sales for this pattern took an upturn as a result."*[13]

*— Jack Alexander*

Capri series, 1954

PINK MILANO

In 1957, the Formica Company released a new pattern designed in-house as a collaboration with the Hurlbut Paper Company. Called *Sequin,* it was another first for the decorative laminate industry: very small chips of gold-colored aluminum lightly scattered on a white paper background. That year, the company expanded and revised the Sunrise Color Line again, unveiling two new Loewy patterns. *Nassau,* a buoyant design of overlapping watercolor shapes, and *Color Grain,* a stylized tone-on-tone wood grain in bright colors were introduced. Also released were several new wood grains in the *Picwood* line, including Teak for the first time. The following year brought additional color options for *Nassau, Sequin,* and *Linen.*

The *Sequin* line was further expanded in 1959 with a marketing campaign centered around the anniversary of the Gold Rush. Sequin's signature gold flecks were available on three pastel color backdrops: Rose Beige, Light Aqua, and pink Camellia. That same year Raymond Loewy Associates curated the CandleGlo Collection which included four new patterns, all in muted earth-tone colors. Created by Nettie Hart, one of Loewy's most important designers, *Frost* appeared as ice crystals on a window pane. *Tidestone* had the look of irregular, weathered rock on a light background. *Parfait*'s light-hearted pattern was evoc-

HONEY BEIGE NASSAU

SEA MIST NASSA

Parfait series, 1959

ative of microscopic amoeba and *Bonbon*'s was composed of multi-colored dots with a sponge paint effect. This mix of whimsical patterns and muted colors was a fitting transition from the 1950s to the changes coming in the 1960s. Raymond Loewy Associates and William Snaith Design Consultants later expanded on *Sequin* in 1962 with *Silversnow*. Rather than gold-colored metal pieces, *Silversnow* had significantly smaller pieces of aluminum in their natural silver floating in fields of solid colors — though it never gained the popularity that the original *Sequin* had.

Color Grain, 1957

GRAY
FROST.171

BEIGE
FROST.172

Frost and Tidestone, 1959-1960

Beauty Bonded
FORMICA
Reg. U.S. Pat. Off
62-J-66

GREEN SILVERS SNOW

Mint Bonbon
63-PD-47

# EUROPEAN CONNECTIONS

In 1946, the Formica Company partnered with the storied British printer De La Rue to begin production in the international market. Founded in 1821 by Thomas De La Rue, the new partner was known for printing everything from stationery and playing cards to stamps and banknotes. The Formica® decorative laminate patterns created in the United States were replicated by local cylinder engravers for production in London, sometimes with minor variations, and new names were assigned, for example, *Pearl* became *Onyx* and *Linen* was called *Linette* in the UK.

Also in the late 1950s, De La Rue met with the textile designer Lucienne Day and furniture designer Robin Day to discuss the possibilities of collaboration. Lucienne and Robin Day were some of the most celebrated designers of the mid-century period and are sometimes referred to as the British equivalents of Ray and Charles Eames. Lucienne had been allowing UK-based furniture manufacturer Kandya Ltd. to use some of her fabric designs to adapt for laminate on their furniture surfaces.[14]

Pantomime samples on top of Pennant, 1959

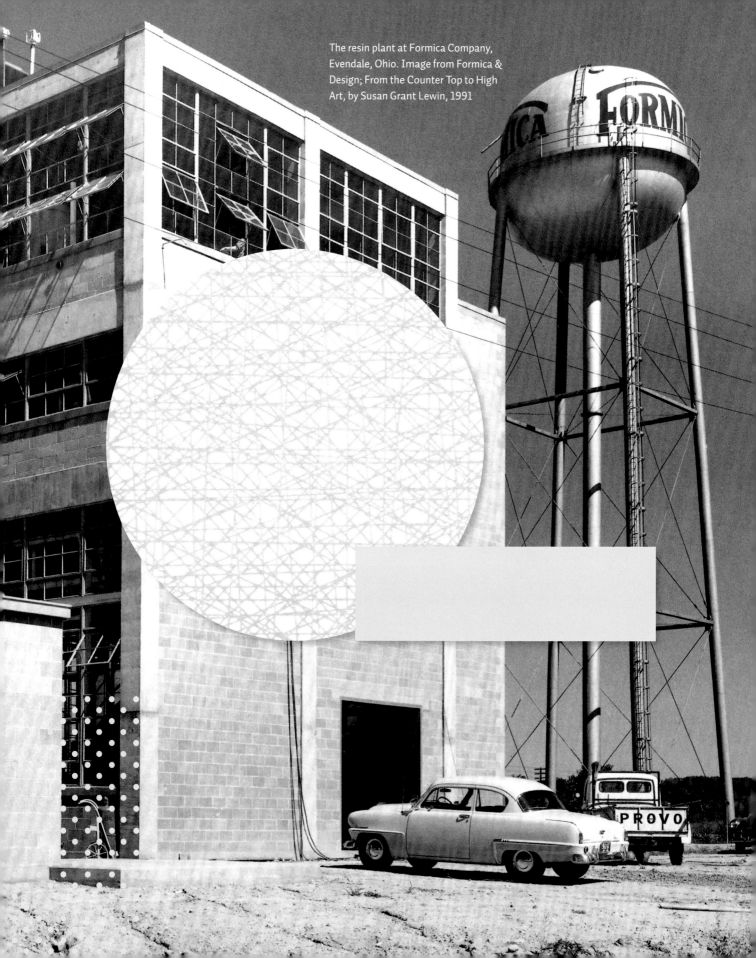

The resin plant at Formica Company, Evendale, Ohio. Image from Formica & Design; From the Counter Top to High Art, by Susan Grant Lewin, 1991

While it is not known if Lucienne Day ever provided any pattern designs to the Formica Company, Robin did produce at least one. In 1959 he was working as a color consultant for Storey's of Lancaster, a manufacturer of plastic home furnishings, and designed *Pennant* for use as a vinyl upholstery for chairs and as a decorative laminate for counters and tabletops, the latter through an agreement with Formica Co./De La Rue. *Pennant* was "composed of fine criss-crossing lines printed in black on a red, blue, yellow, or white ground" and was reportedly Robin's first foray into pattern design.[15]

De La Rue released *Pennant* within the UK, along with other patterns it developed separately from the Formica Company's collections at the time. In 1959, they introduced the designs *Pantomime*, *Gondola*, *Pompadour*, and *Leaf*. *Pantomime* was a geometric pattern of triangles forming diamonds and *Gondola* was a graphic pattern with bowed lines over rectangular shapes. *Pompadour* had a complex woven appearance and *Leaf* featured hand-drawn maple leaves floating over lighter versions of the same.

Meanwhile, a competing brand in Sweden called Perstorp released *VirrVarr* in 1958. Its complex pattern of overlapping lines was designed by Count Sigvard Bernadotte, the son of the King of Sweden at the time and one of Sweden's most influential industrial designers. Perstorp would later be acquired by the Formica Group and *VirrVarr* would be brought into the company's library.

VirrVarr series, 1958

> By the 1950s "Formica laminate had become a technically mature product; it subsequently changed little. Its surface designs changed frequently, however, encompassing not only plastic's traditional function of imitation but also suggesting the American culture's fascination with endlessly remolding a malleable environment."
>
> — Jeffrey L. Meikle[16]

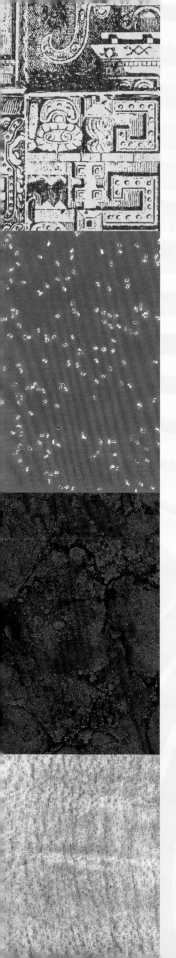

# CHAPTER THREE

# 1960s & 1970s

**T**he relative stability and optimism of the late 40s and 50s gave way to two decades largely defined by social upheaval and political turmoil. In the 1960s and 1970s, the counterculture and social movements fought for civil rights for minorities and women, while the United States sent soldiers to Vietnam and accelerated the Cold War with the Space Race. The birth control pill was approved by the FDA in 1960, contributing to the rise of the Women's Liberation movement and more opportunities for women. NASA's Apollo program sparked new thought in the population at large; Apollo 8's image of planet Earth planted the seed for a vocal environmental movement, while Apollo 11's lunar landing rallied the entire populace around the triumph of human achievement. Meanwhile, the energy crisis in 1973, the Watergate scandal of 1974, and the U.S.

Vanitory Design Portfolio illustrated by
Jeremiah Goodman, 1965

Formica Corporation

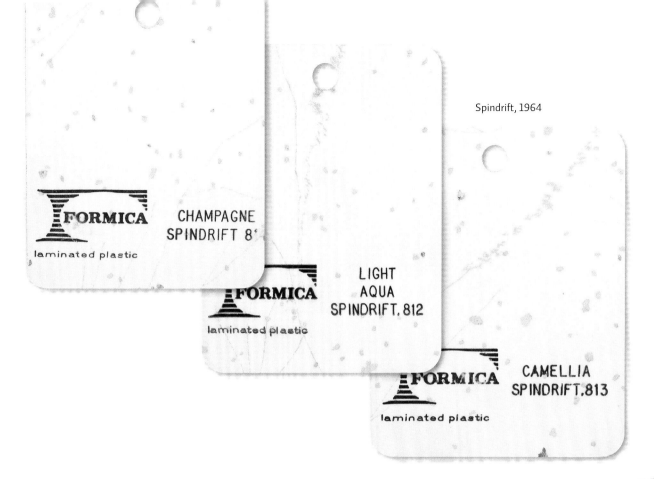

FORMICA
laminated plastic
CHAMPAGNE
SPINDRIFT 8¹

FORMICA
laminated plastic
LIGHT
AQUA
SPINDRIFT. 812

FORMICA
laminated plastic
CAMELLIA
SPINDRIFT.813

Spindrift, 1964

withdrawal from Vietnam in 1975 were hallmarks of a time riddled with polarization, uncertainty, and discontent.

That tension manifested itself in the design philosophies of the day; the strict rules and sometimes-misguided idealism of Modernism (think: monochromaticity, derivative skyscrapers, and tabula rasa urban renewal) led to countermovements by the 1960s and 1970s including Pop Art, Deconstructivism, and Postmodernism. By the mid-60s, interior design and fashion moved away from the romantic pastel hues of the previous era and toward psychedelic colors and also autumnal shades of a more muted, earthy character. The Formica Company's International Design Award-winning Citation Series in 1964 had a veritable rainbow of colors including Bittersweet, Caribbean Blue, Grape, Lemon Twist, Lime, and Raspberry — reflecting the popularity of kaleidoscopic brights at the time. However, this collection was primarily for the commercial market and residential patterns and colors remained largely in muted colors and natural patterns during this period. Popular kitchen colors of the period included many shades of brown along with Avocado green, Harvest Gold yellow, and Burnt Sienna orange.

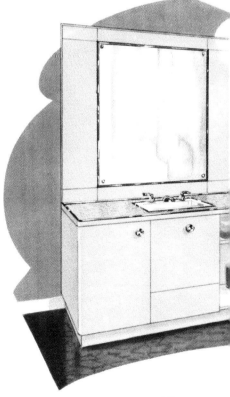

GRAY
LINEN, 101

ed plastic

TAN
LINEN, 103

laminated plastic

LIPSTICK
RED
LINEN, 105

laminated plastic

GREEN
LINEN, 106

plastic

PRIMROSE
LINEN, 107

laminated plastic

POWDER
BLUE
LINEN, 108

laminated plastic

WEXFORD
IRISH LINEN
160

plastic

NATURAL
IRISH LINEN
161-(30)

laminated plastic

HARVEST GOLD
IRISH LINEN
165 (-30)

laminated plastic

CHARCOAL LINEN

Beauty Bonded
FORMICA
Reg. U.S. Pat. Off.
6-C-70

Beauty Bonded
FORMICA
Reg. U.S. Pat. Off.
2-C-1

GRAY LINEN

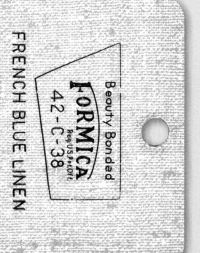

Beauty Bonded
FORMICA
Reg. U.S. Pat. Off.
42-C-38

FRENCH BLUE LINEN

Beauty Bonded
FORMICA
Reg. U.S. Pat. Off.
32-C-1

PETAL PINK LINEN

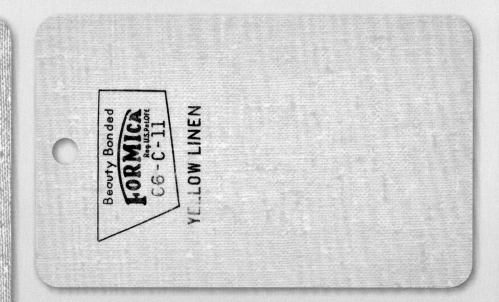

Beauty Bonded
FORMICA
Reg. U.S. Pat. Off.
6-C-11

YELLOW LINEN

47

FORMICA® MONTEZUMA
BRAND 7405
laminated plastic

64 SUEDE

Montezuma, part of the Formica Special Designs

# IN-HOUSE DESIGNERS TAKE THE LEAD

By the late 1950s, the Formica Company design team was beginning to create more patterns in-house, without the use of consultants. To reflect its reinvestment in the design effort, the Formica Co. built an 80,000 sq. ft. Research and Design Center in Evendale in 1960. During this period, the company had the capacity to silk-screen at the Winton Place plant and the designers, lead by artist Jack Willard created custom patterns. Called Formica Special Designs, they were created for the commercial market "for a dramatic change of pace in surface treatment [and] for controlled emphasis." A series of 32 silk-screened patterns available in customizable colors and backgrounds, they included designs as varied as the highly-detailed pencil drawings based on Aztec stone carvings called *Montezuma* to the refined De Stijl simplicity of *Mondrian*. The silk-screening equipment was removed from the Winton Place plant and relocated to a new facility in California in 1966 and the custom lines were discontinued in the U.S. in 1969 (the French office continued to produce them in the decades to come).[17]

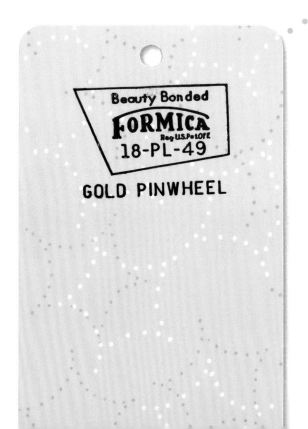

**Beauty Bonded**
**FORMICA**
Reg. U.S. Pat. Off.
18-PL-49

GOLD PINWHEEL

**Beauty Bonded**
**FORMICA**
Reg. U.S. Pat. Off.
2-PL-1

WHITE PINWHEEL

PEARL ONDINE
700 – (60)

BLUE (
702

FORMICA
BRAND

Ondine series, 1963

WHITE TIDEWOOD

Released in 1961 and most likely designed in-house, *Flamenco* was a pattern similar to the geometries of Islamic architecture and *Pinwheel* was a subtle pattern of dots creating overlapping star shapes. In 1963, in-house engineers and designers created *Ondine*, a marbled paper-style pattern using a flotation method whereby paint and oil were mixed into a shallow bath of water and then the decór paper was gently dipped onto the surface so that no two pieces were the same. That year the Formica Company team also released *Tidewood* which had the look of whitewashed and weathered Rosewood grain and *Finesse*, likely a later variation of *Softglo*. The following year, *Spindrift* and *Mayflower* were released. Designed by the company's first professional in-house pattern designer, Lorraine Elton, *Spindrift* used a combination of cracks and scratches with *Sequin*'s glittery flecks to create a unique pattern reportedly inspired by the concrete floor of the company's historic manufacturing plant. *Mayflower* used repeating designs of hand-drawn flowers with occasional variations of color or overlayed shape.

Flamenco, 1961

SAUTERNE
SOLID
FINESSE, 261

CANDLELITE
SOLID
FINESSE, 262

FORMICA

MOONWHITE
SOLID
FINESSE, 263

PINEMIST
SOLID
FINESSE, 266

FORMICA

68

Mayflower, 1964

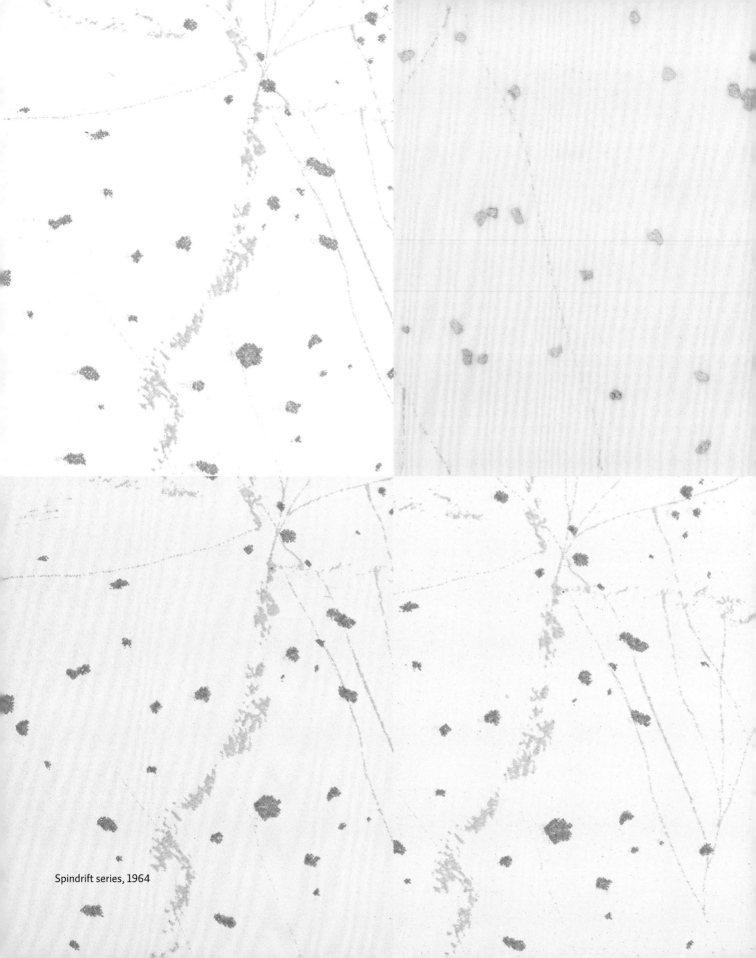

Spindrift series, 1964

World's Fair House Sweepstakes
advertisement, 1965

# 1964 WORLD'S FAIR

The Formica Company made a splashy entry into the 1964 New York World's Fair, reaching beyond the typical exhibit and creating an entire house to show off the possibilities of Formica decorative laminate. Called The World's Fair House, the Ranch style home was outfitted with Formica laminate in every room, from countertops and cabinets to wall paneling and custom furniture designed by Leo Jiranek. Not only did the "Formica House" expose thousands of visitors to new ideas in laminate, but more than 100 variations of the house plan were built by developers in cities across 41 states and the Formica Company published a book on the project, garnering enormous attention in publications coast-to-coast. Raymond Loewy Associates contributed many unique patterns for the exhibit's surfaces, though only a few found their way into production after the fair. One was *Delta*, a geometric pattern reminiscent of South Pacific prints.

1964 Laminated painting of New York World's Fair, Formica Group Private Collection

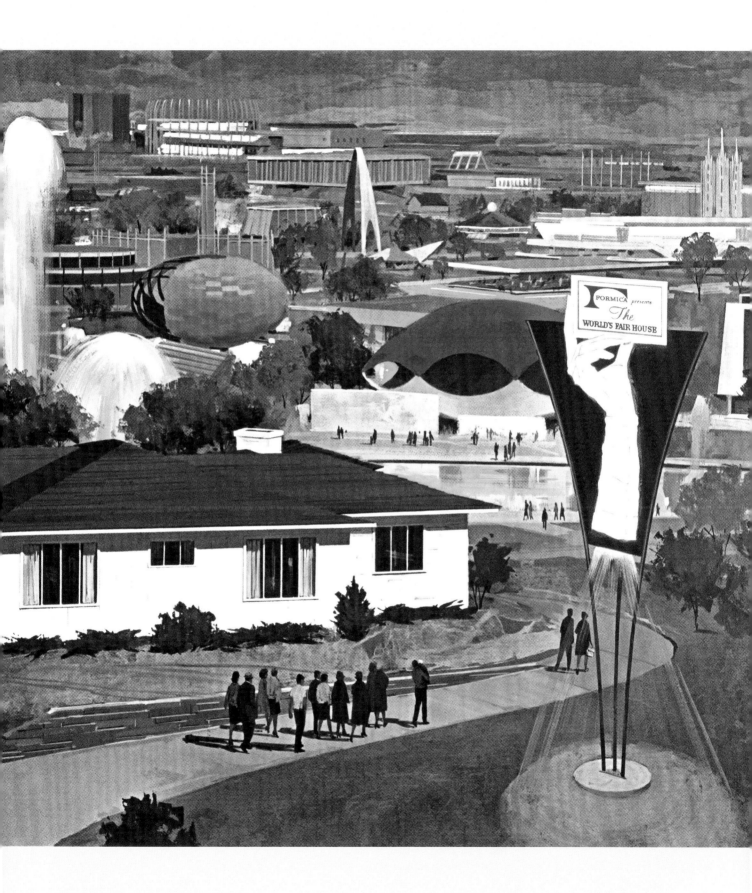

The World's Fair House
program, 1964

58

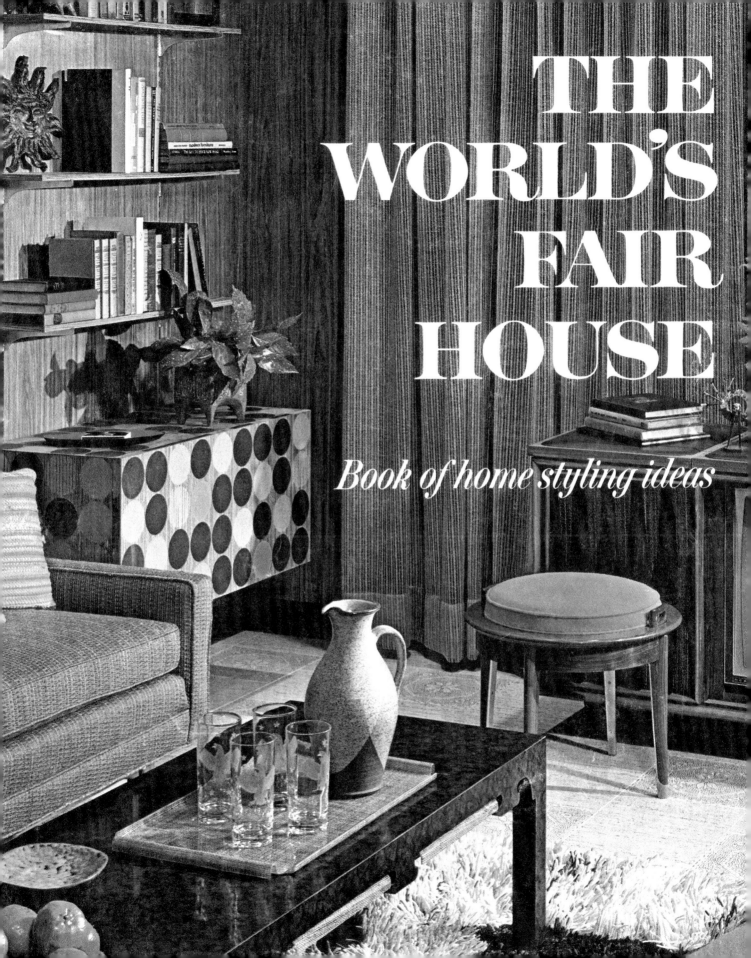

# THE WORLD'S FAIR HOUSE

*Book of home styling ideas*

Pink Linen

Gray Linen
2-C-1

*(Skylark swatch — partial label)* Skylark

White Skylark
90-L-1

Spindrift

White Spindrift
11-S-1

Sequin

White Sequin
28-SE-1

White
949

Beige

Antique White
132

SK    New Decorator Ideas book,
date unknown

# FORMICA DESIGN STUDIO

The company created its first official "art department," the Design Studio, in 1965 in a renovated portion of the historic Winton Place plant in Cincinnati and hired more designers to join Lorraine Elton. Bob Ford was already working for the company in the Engineering Department at that time and moved into the Design Studio while Sharon de Leon was a new hire. That same year, Bob Ford created *Willow*, based on the trees of architectural plans, and the company also released a new version of *Fernglo*. Still based on leaves, the new *Fernglo* foliage was at a smaller scale and more iconographic than the 1954 version.

Also in 1965, Bob Ford and others at the company worked with the artist Jeremiah Goodman to create a marketing booklet that showed laminate used on bathroom vanities and dressing tables. At the time, Jeremiah Goodman was Interior Design magazine's longtime illustrator and had painted portraits of the homes of stars like Bob Hope. The illustrations in Goodman's trademark sensuous watercolors helped inspire and inform designers, fabricators, and homeowners about the myriad decorating styles in which Formica® laminate worked seamlessly.

Sharon de Leon began contributing to the Formica Company's story before she had even been hired. During her job interview, the team was so drawn to a design from her portfolio that the company purchased the rights and began preparing cylinders before Sharon's employment contract was even finalized! The resulting pattern was named *Halifax*, an elaborate hand-drawn matrix of various small rectangular and sunburst shapes, released in 1966. The original colors included Sage, Amber, and Beige to coincide with the rising popularity of green (Avocado) and yellow-orange (Harvest Gold) appliances and earth-toned interiors. For Expo 67 in Montreal, the company released The Collection of 67 which featured 67 new colors. Two plant-inspired patterns released at that time included the superimposed hand-drawn flowers of *Fleurette* and the pressed foliage or cyanotype style of *Pastoral*. Lorraine Elton designed an ephemeral, cloud-like pattern called *Gossamer* in 1968 — appropriately released in Avocado and Gold.

60

GREEN
WILLOW.782

Willow, 1965 and Pastorale, 1967

Halifax series, 1966

by **FORMICA**®

New Decorator Ideas book, date unknown

Fleurette series, 1967

Meanwhile, because the West Coast was seeing such dramatic population growth, the Formica Corporation built its second manufacturing facility, the Sierra Plant, outside Sacramento, California in 1966. A second Formica Design Studio was established in Los Angeles soon thereafter. During this period, the company joined a national trade organization, the Color Marketing Group, to help guide and coordinate colors in appliances and other products. This was key to creating decorative laminates in colors and patterns that would be marketable for homes and businesses, especially in an era of economic uncertainty when buyers wanted durable goods that would stay relevant as long as possible. In 1969, the company's design and research components were expanded. A new Design Center was built on the Evendale campus and the previous building was renamed the Research & Development Center, adding equipment to make samples for on-site testing and evaluation. By 1970 the company had ceased all industrial laminate production, thus focusing solely on the decorative laminates it pioneered.[18]

The next decade featured decidedly natural patterns. 1970 saw the release of *Gemini*, an array of abstracted flowers, and *Grasscloth*, likely created using a print of actual woven seagrass. Originally created for commercial furniture applications, *Desk* was also released in 1970 and had the appearance of a fine, woven fabric. The timeless look of *Butcherblock* came out in 1972. Designed in-house by Bob Ford, *Butcherblock* was available for nearly 50 years, retiring in 2022. *Fire Agate* came out in 1973 and appeared like cut volcanic rock; then *Celestial* in 1974 evoked the look of mottled stone or oxidized metal.

A field of lightly-sponged paint with a very subtle grid of squares, *Mosaic* was designed in-house in 1975. That year, the company also created the International Collection—consisting of various realistic wood grains including varieties such as *Finnish Oak*, *Island Koa*, *Asian Teak*, and *Colonial Cherry*. *Firedance*, which had the appearance of hot lava, came out in 1976. In 1979, Bob Ford was inspired by the genuine leather of Jaguar automobiles when creating *Papyrus*. Finally, the company released a second edition of the International Collection called Series II — Naturals, which included a deep physical texture to add realism to natural patterns such as *Woven Grass*, *Basket Cane*, *Striped Cork*, and *Bronze Tile*.

FORMICA® BRAND
laminated plastic

GEMINI WHITE
740 (-30)

FORMICA ®
BRAND
minated plastic

GEMINI GOLD
741 (-30)

FORMICA ®
BRAND
laminated plastic

GEMINI WHITE
740 (-30)

FORMICA
BRAND
laminate

211
Beige
Mosaic
MATTE FINISH

FORMICA
BRAND
laminate

210
Gray
Mosaic
MATTE FINISH

FORMICA
BRAND
laminate

718
Moonstone
Papyrus
MATTE FINISH

FORMICA
BRAND
laminate

717
Seafrost
Papyrus
MATTE FINISH

67

Natural Collection Brochure, 1982

BUTCHERBLOCK
OAK
DESIGI
-58 F

ERTICAL GRADE

CHERBLOCK
MAPLE
58 FINISH
IN
AIN
E

FORMICA®
BRAND
laminate
© FORMICA CORPORATION

7142 AMBER

Butcherblock series, 1972

69

MICA

## 117
Colonial MICA
Cherry
MATTE FIN
View Larger S

## 116
Asian
Teak
MATTE F
View Larger
MICA

## 118
Finnish
Oak
MATTE FINISH
View Larger Sampl

FIREDANCE
DESIGN-242
-58 FINISH

FORMICA
laminated plastic

FORMICA
decorative laminate

COPPER
CELESTIAL
DESIGN-280
-90 FINISH

VIEW LARGER SAMPLE BEFORE PURCHASE

Fire Agate, 1973

FO
products

APPROVED
DATE ____
CUSTOMER
FINISH ____

# DESIGN ADVISORY BOARD

In 1974, the Formica Corporation created the Design Advisory Board, a think tank composed of some of the most influential architects and designers, to "explore new directions in laminate design."[19] The commercial sector was the company's fastest-growing market and creating a dialogue with the design industry was crucial to successful product lines and marketing. Interior designers included Joseph Paul D'Urso, Margaret Larcade, William (Billy) McCarty-Cooper, Tony Moses, Charles Morris Mount, Barbara Ross, Valerian S. Rybar, John Saladino, Barbara Schwartz, and Mary Wolter. Architects included Charles Boxenbaum, Alan Buchsbaum, Richard W. Hobbs, Paul Segal, Donald Singer, and William Turnbull, Jr. Joining them were product designer Ristomatti Ratia of Marimekko and industrial designer Bob Blaich of Philips.[20]

The Design Advisory Board signaled a shift for the company toward research and development in new applications and possibilities for laminate, at a time when competition from other materials was becoming increasingly fierce. By the

| **Charles Boxenbaum** | **Alan Buchsbaum** | **Joseph Paul D'Urso** | **Mary Wolter** | | **Richard W. Hobbs** | **Donald Singer** | **Margaret Larcade** | **Tony Moses** | **Billy McCarty** |
|---|---|---|---|---|---|---|---|---|---|
| A New York architect who also is registered in Israel, Charles Boxenbaum, A.I.A., received his Bachelor of Architecture degree from Pratt Institute and his Master of Architecture from Harvard University. His practice consists mainly of residential and small commercial work and the design of furniture and lighting for individual and production pieces. He has taught at Rensselaer Polytechnic Institute, and served as visiting critic at a number of other schools of architecture. | Born in Savannah, Georgia, Alan Buchsbaum is a graduate of Georgia Tech and received his Bachelor of Architecture degree from Massachusetts Institute of Technology. He is a partner in Design Coalition, New York architects whose work includes new residential construction as well as interior renovations. Buchsbaum has had broad experience in exhibit, graphic and product design and has been the recipient of several design awards. | A pioneer in the use of industrial materials, furnishings and equipment for residential use, Joe D'Urso is known for his architectural use of space with minimal furnishings and a minimal palette. He received his B.A. in Interior Design from Pratt Institute and his M.A. in Fine Arts from Manchester College of Art and Design, Manchester, England. He has won several awards in interior design and is Adjunct Professor of Design at Pratt Institute. | Mary Wolter is an interiors coordinator for Schwartzman & Tucci Consultants, Inc., New York, a design firm specializing in store planning. As a consultant in color and materials, Wolter has been involved in the planning of stores for all the major department store chains. She received her Bachelor of Design and Masters of Interior Design at the University of Michigan. | | Richard W. Hobbs, A.I.A., is a Partner in Hobbs Fukui Associates, a Seattle architectural firm which, since its formation in 1968, has received numerous professional design awards. Hobbs has been involved in the design of low-cost, cluster and multiple-family housing units, interior space planning, site and feasibility studies, comprehensive master planning, commercial facilities, as well as custom private residences. He received his Bachelor of Architecture from the University of Washington and his Master of Science in Architecture from Columbia University. | A Fort Lauderdale, Florida architect, Donald Singer, A.I.A., has received a total of fourteen professional design awards since 1965 and was one of a select few architects whose work was included in the U.S. Information Agency traveling exhibit "Architecture U.S.A." He received his Bachelor of Architecture from the University of Florida and his Master of Architecture from Columbia University. He has designed a variety of projects ranging from volume and interiors of private residences to a master plan for Nova University's Oceanographic Research Laboratory. | Interior Design Partner for Lance, Larcade and Bechtol, architects and interior designers in San Antonio, Texas, Margaret Larcade is a color specialist known for her exciting use of color against neutral backgrounds. Born in Detroit, Michigan, she is a graduate of Syracuse University and the New York School of Interior Design. Her commitment to contemporary architecture, design, furniture and art is reflected in all her projects. | A graduate of the Maryland Institute College of Art in Baltimore, Tony Moses recently moved his office, TM Design Studio, to New York City. He specializes in interior and environmental design for low, middle and above middle income clients. He has designed furniture, wallcoverings, accessories, supergraphics and displays. | With an interior business that c regularly betwe York and Lond McCarty also d wallcoverings, carpets and fu The winner of s sign awards in Wallcovering c Award in 1971 tended the Uni Pennsylvania S Fine Arts and s history and crit the Barnes Fou Merion, Penns |

late 70s, the company's attention was focused more on the commercial market and the needs of designers. In 1978, the U.S. Federal Trade Commission filed a motion to cancel the Formica brand's trademark, arguing that the word "Formica" had become a generic term. The action was later dropped, protecting Formica decorative laminate's reputation as the authentic original.

*"Without the designer working with the manufacturer, we could face a future where building products meet manufacturing expediency only, resulting in dull and uninspired environments."*

— Design Advisory Board[21]

| **Charles Morris Mount** | **Barbara Ross** | **John Saladino** | **Paul Segal** | **Barbara Schwartz** | **Ristomatti Ratia** | **William Turnbull, Jr.** | **Valerian S. Rybar** |
|---|---|---|---|---|---|---|---|
| A leading restaurant and kitchen designer, Charles Mount has also designed such diverse projects as a department store for children and a law center and library for the Arkansas Bar Association. Born in Brantley, Alabama, Mount received his degree in interior design from Auburn University. He attended the Memphis Academy of Arts in Memphis, Tennessee and the Ecole des Beaux Arts in Fontainebleau, France. | Barbara Ross is a Partner and Vice President of Dexter Design, Inc., a New York based interior design firm. A graduate of Pratt Institute with a Bachelor of Fine Arts, she is a member of the Architectural League and a sponsor of the Institute of Architecture and Urban Studies. A specialist in color theory, she is writing a book on the emotional and psychological impact of colors in the home environment. | John Saladino is best known for having mastered the seemingly impossible—minimal interiors that are breathtakingly luxurious at the same time. A graduate of the University of Notre Dame with a Bachelor of Fine Arts, Saladino received his Master of Fine Arts at Yale University School of Art and Architecture. Born in Kansas City, Missouri, he heads his own interior design firm in New York City which handles both residential and corporate clients. | The Principal of Paul Segal Associates, a New York architectural firm, Paul Segal, A.I.A., received his Bachelor of Arts and Master of Fine Arts in Architecture from Princeton University. He has been a guest critic in design at Columbia, Princeton and Cooper Union, and developed and taught a course, funded by the Ford Foundation through E.F.L., on participatory environmental design for high school students. He is the recipient of several professional awards for both residential and commercial design. | Barbara Schwartz is a graduate of the State University of New York and the New York School of Interior Design. A Partner and President of Dexter Design, Inc., she is a member of A.S.I.D., a Junior Council member of the Museum of Modern Art, a Vice President of the Merce Cunningham Dance Foundation, and Chairperson of several Whitney Museum committees. | Ristomatti Ratia is creative vice president of Marimekko, the Finnish firm which pioneered the design of brilliant contemporary printed fabrics. The 1977 Tommy Award winner for best design for his "Happy" sheet pattern, Ratia now resides in the United States. He has designed numerous residential and commercial interiors both here and in Finland and also designs furniture. He is a graduate of the Helsinki School of Business and England's Leicester School of Art where he studied interior and product design. | A designer of the world-renowned California "Sea Ranch" condominiums, William Turnbull, F.A.I.A., holds 32 national and regional awards for design excellence. Currently heading his own firm in San Francisco, and on the Architectural Faculty of the University of California, Berkeley, he received his Bachelor of Fine Arts and Master of Fine Arts in Architecture from Princeton University and attended the Ecole des Beaux Arts de Fontainebleau. He has been on seven A.I.A. Honor Award Juries, including the National Award Jury in 1969 and 1976. | Internationally renowned interior designer, with offices in New York and Paris, Valerian Rybar is responsible for numerous trends in the design field including the use of stainless steel, chrome and brass in interior detailing, flooring and bathroom fixtures. His work is particularly known for its profound understanding of architecture, his inventive space planning, his attention to detail and his innovative use of traditional and contemporary materials. Born, educated in Europe, he was headed for a diplomatic career and studied law prior to entering the field of interior design in the U.S. |

Design Advisory brochure, 1981

 MEDICI
7419

laminated plastic

- 64 SUEDE

  MALTESE
CROSS
7409

laminated plastic

Formica Specialty Designs, 1960-1969

 **FORMICA**® BRAND

laminated plastic

LES PLUMES
RED
7425B

- 64 SUEDE

 **FORMICA**® BRAND

laminated plastic

MANTILLA
7404

- 64 SUEDE

# CHAPTER FOUR

# 1980s & 1990s

**T**he 1980s kicked off yet another period of economic growth and rapid advances in technology. Home computers, video game consoles, boomboxes, and VCRs became widely available during this era and by the 1990s, access to the internet was becoming common in American homes. Popular television series of the decades such as *Cheers, Family Ties, Friends,* and *The Fresh Prince of Bel-Air* highlighted the importance of family and community. Music artists including Madonna, Michael Jackson, Whitney Houston, and Boyz II Men represent the youthful energy of the period.

As part of the larger Postmodern movement and its reaction to the strict rules of modernism, Memphis (an informal design collective) was founded in Milan in 1981. Memphis influenced design trends throughout the 1980s with

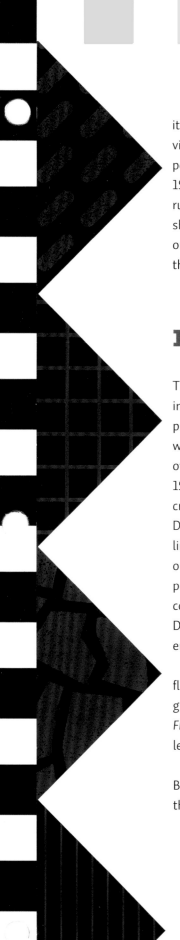

its bold geometric forms, playful graphics, and kaleidoscopic color palette. The vibrant and glowing colors of disco, MTV, and video games also influenced the period's bright hues like hot pink, turquoise, electric blue, and yellow. By the 1990s, colors began to fade in intensity leading to softer shades like slate blue, rust, brown, and mauve with neutrals as the new standard. Kitchen appliances shifted away from color and were produced primarily in Almond, Bisque, black or white throughout the 80s and 90s, and then eventually in stainless steel by the end of the millennium.

# DESIGN CONCEPTS

The Formica Company built a Press Plate production plant in Quillan, France in 1964. Still the only manufacturer of decorative laminate with in-house plate production today, it provided designers and technicians the ability to experiment with using texture to create pattern. By developing a method of using variations of texture and gloss on a solid color, the Design Concepts line was created in 1980 by the French office of Formica Group, based on the recommendations and creative input of the Design Advisory Board and with curation by Formica Group Design Director Alessandro (Alex) De Gregori. Patterns in the Design Concepts line included *Flip, Maxi Graph, Rock,* and *Pin Stripe*. All were made using solid colored paper and had textural patterns resembling rows of pill shapes, graph paper, stone pavers, and suit fabric, respectively. Available in nine greyscales and colors including slate blue Colonial, hunter green Nile, and burgundy Cordovan, Design Concepts was awarded Best in Show at the Institute of Business Designers' Product Design Competition.[22]

In 1980, Bob Ford designed *Woodland*, a dense layer of foliage on a forest floor. Three years later, Formica Group designers created *Optix*, an ultra-small grid pattern with soft lines that could be seen as a modern update to *Linen*. *Flora*, a Bob Ford pattern inspired by vintage French botanical prints, was released in 1987.

In 1983 and 1984, Postmodern pioneers Robert Venturi and Denise Scott Brown designed a custom silk screen pattern to be printed on laminate for the bentwood furniture in Knoll's Venturi Collection. The collection featured

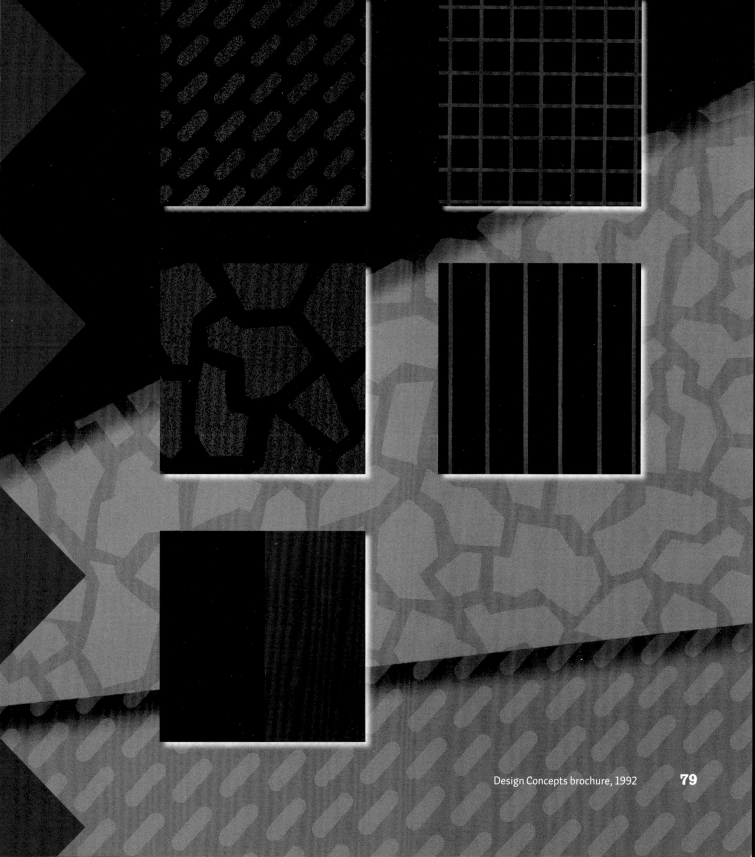

Design Concepts brochure, 1992 **79**

Woodland series, 1980
Optix series, 1983
Flora series, 1987

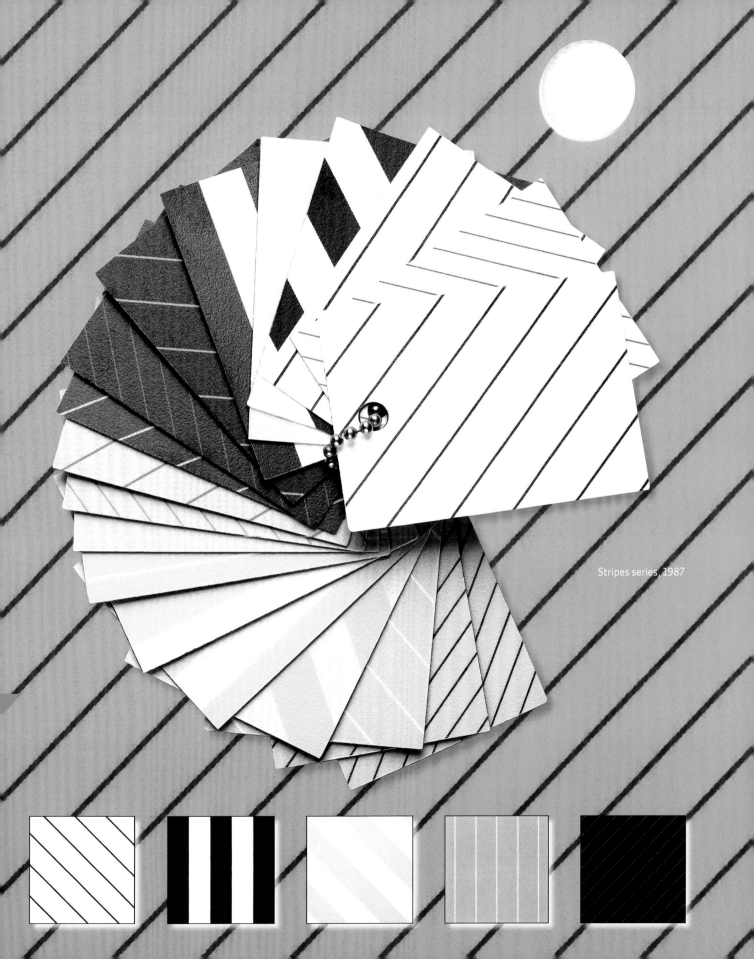

Stripes series, 1987

abstracted and "flattened" versions of classic chair styles. The Queen Anne and Chippendale chairs featured the playful pattern of a floral background in soft colors and a matrix of double black lines rotated above. On the use of pattern in the collection, Venturi noted, "it's a way of getting richness, because I think the aesthetic ideal of today is one of richness over unity, so using pattern is important."[23]

Until the mid-1980s, the Formica Corporation had its own in-house rotogravure printing facilities in the plants in Cincinnati, France, Spain, and the UK. This created a close relationship between the pattern designers and the engravers during design and production. Starting around 1985, the company began outsourcing the rotogravure printing to suppliers so the connection shifted to one between the Formica Group designers and the designers at each partner supplier. The added capacity allowed for increased pattern development and creative collaborations between various design teams, a unique and fruitful relationship that exists to this day.

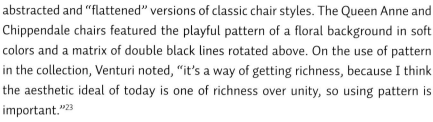

"In the present postmodern era, characterized by a commitment to surface and to the superficial in all the senses, Formica laminate is a material without par. By both covering and revealing, and by showing a remarkable commitment to depth in its thin surface, Formica laminate has not simply weathered the trend toward layering and eclecticism, it has been integral to it. Its ability to be whatever we want it to be has made Formica laminate an uncommon material."

— Steven Holt[24]

Formica catalog, 1987

Photograph of prototype sample featuring
Venturi Pattern in Formica Archives

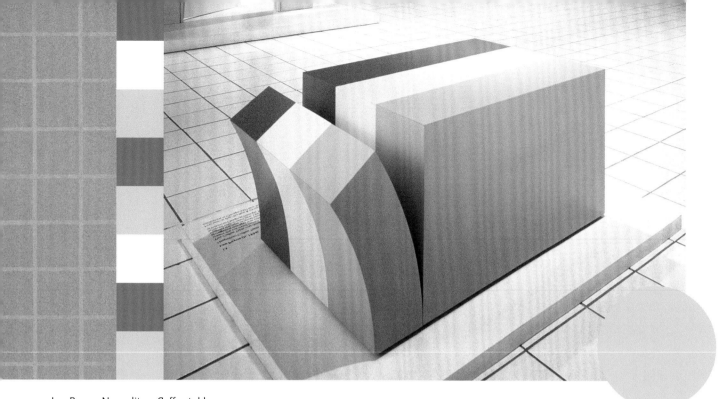

Lee Payne, Neapolitan. Coffee table exhibition of ColorCore® Laminate from exhibition site, 1983

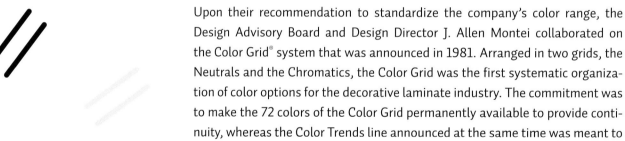

# FOCUS ON COLOR

Upon their recommendation to standardize the company's color range, the Design Advisory Board and Design Director J. Allen Montei collaborated on the Color Grid® system that was announced in 1981. Arranged in two grids, the Neutrals and the Chromatics, the Color Grid was the first systematic organization of color options for the decorative laminate industry. The commitment was to make the 72 colors of the Color Grid permanently available to provide continuity, whereas the Color Trends line announced at the same time was meant to change from year to year.

Another first came in 1982 — ColorCore®, a patented solid color product. Rather than a thin decorative layer and a dark edge, ColorCore was colored through and through allowing the edge to be exposed. It was available in all 108 solids of Color Grid and Color Trends and became an immediate sensation in the design community. Extensive marketing helped; by 1985 it was noted that eighty percent of architects and designers were aware of ColorCore. The focus on variety and standardization of color was understandable given the era's multi-chromatic trends. In 1983, the Formica company partnered with the Art Institute of Chicago on a design competition entitled Surface and Ornament. Exhibited in 1984, invited artists and designers including Frank Gehry, Ward Bennett, Charles Moore, Robert Venturi, Denise Scott Brown, and Helmut Jahn created original works using ColorCore.[25]

"Colorcore-dinated kitchen," designed by L.A. artist Peter Shire, date unknown. Press release image, Formica Archives

85

# 75TH ANNIVERSARY

To commemorate the company's 75th anniversary, Formica Corporation Creative Director Susan Grant Lewin held a reception and product launch in the Rainbow Room at Rockefeller Center on May 24, 1988. In celebration, the company's beloved *Skylark* was renamed *Boomerang* and released in four colors including Charcoal, Grecian Blue, Rosetta, and White. Styled by Alex De Gregori, *Boomerang* was printed in the Formica Group France plant using their rotary silk screen capabilities.

Tibor Kalman, the graphic designer and founder of New York firm M&Co., was hired to reorganize Formica Corporation's solid color portfolio and made a presentation at the anniversary event. Called COLOR+COLOR, the line included 108 colors — 80 existing and 28 new — organized into six families (red, orange, yellow, green, blue, and black & white) and then further sorted by brightness, value, and texture.

Alex De Gregori released a few new patterns in 1989. These included *Granito*, a fine-grained granite pattern over colors hand-chosen to complement the contemporary palette, including yellow Curry, turquoise Dusty Jade, and pink Rose Ash. The other patterns were *Papercraft*, which had the appearance of handmade paper, and *Milano Stripe*, subtle diagonal striations with the occasional pastel accents in pink, turquoise, and yellow. The same year, Formica Group designers collaborated with Herman Miller designer Bill Lausch on the *Frosted Series* as the industry had begun experimenting with using optical solids rather than wood grains for systems office furniture.

Milano Stripe series, 1989

**FORMICA®** BRAND
laminate

# 664
# NEO PAPERCRAFT
## MATTE FINISH

Papercraft series, 1989

# FORMATIONS COLLECTION

1989 saw the introduction of the Formations Collection, styled by Alex De Gregori. The collection included various patterns, all inspired by sand and stone, including *Grafix*, *Dust*, *Oxide*, *Patina*, *Volcano*, and the previously-released *Granito*. They ranged in scale and complexity with *Grafix* being the smallest grain and *Volcano* the largest. The launch featured a unique brochure that unfolded to reveal a large spiral of patterns and colors, organized to illustrate the design concept of scale and coordination. The Formations Collection was printed in Japan where the highest quality presses were available at the time. Diana Marra, a Formica Corporation employee in the technical department, moved into the Design Department and spent considerable time in Japan overseeing production of the Formations decór paper.

In 1992, the Formations Collection expanded to include *Scorpio* which fell between Oxide and Patina on the scale. De Gregori wrote that research had "resulted in Formations, a comprehensive open system of solid colors coordinated with dimensional gradations of abstract patterns on laminates. The narrative in this case is the message of aging versus timelessness that is communicated by the interaction of elements and materials with naturalistic references to pattern, color, and scale. This integration of scale with pattern and color was an industry first. Formations leads as a design model for the development of a pattern language capable of renewing the communicative power of the surface of today's pluralistic environment."[26]

Formations Collection brochure, 1992

FORMICA® BRAND laminate

258
RUSSET SCORPIO
MATTE FINISH

Ebony Oxide, 1992

In 1991, DeGregori curated a collection of patterns from the company's European divisions for release in the United States. Called simply European Editions, the collection included designs created in France, Spain, Germany, and the UK. They included *Crimble*, *Galaxia*, *Lacque Metallique*, *Mineral*, and *Stripes* along with faux marble and painted wood grains. *Network* and *Mine* were added to the European Editions a year later. Formica also introduced four subtle patterns in pastel shades in 1992 including the mottled *Fleck*, the dry brush effect of *Brushing*, the recycled paper look of *Fiber*, and the softly crazed finish of *Crackle*.

European Editions, 1991

Lacque Metallique
series, 1991

# REFRACTIONS AND PHANTOMS COLLECTIONS

Then in 1993, Formica Corporation introduced the Refractions Collection, a collaboration between the American and French offices. De Gregori announced the new collection stating they had used "unique printing techniques and precious reflective pigments that glow with the soft, indirect light of the cosmos." The 19 new designs included light and space-inspired patterns such as *Aurora, Chroma, Cosmic, Diffusion, Fusion, Galaxia, Glow, Photon, Quantum, Quasar, Shimmer,* and *Strobe.* Many of the Refractions patterns used special reflective additives in the print ink.

At the same time, the company released the imported Phantoms Collection which was created by the French office as an expansion of their Design Concepts line. Using black-on-black variations in texture to create pattern, the Phantoms Collection included five designs. *Topmatt* had a fine-grained matte texture for a velvety feel while *Plaster* had the appearance of a hand-troweled finish. With small hexagonal shapes spread intermittently over its surface, *Meteore* had the look of sparkling stone. *Spark* and *Shock* both used glossy abstract shapes on matte backgrounds "with an effect reminiscent of a rain-slicked road at night, their beauty transform[ed] the most ordinary surface."[27]

Refractions Collections, 1993

FORMICA® BRAND laminate

Black Quasar, 1993

FORMICA® BRAND
laminate

FORMICA BRAND
laminate

7165-91
GOLDEN SHIMMER
LACQUER FINISH

7169-91
QUANTUM SKY
LACQUER FINISH

7166-91
QUANTUM SAND
LACQUER FINISH

**683 ROSE ASH GRANITO** MATTE FINISH

**DUSTY JADE GRANITO** MATTE FINISH

**CURRY GRANITO** MATTE FINISH

# LAURINDA SPEAR COLLECTION

Architect Laurinda H. Spear, the co-founder of Miami-based firm Arquitectonica, collaborated with Formica Group designers on a line of patterns in 1997. The Laurinda Spear Collection featured eclectic designs with intertwining patterns and themes organized into four series. For the Rainforest Series, Laurinda worked with children to contribute simple art and she learned of their fears related to the depletion of the rainforest for monetary gain. *For Rent* used newsprint from the four regions of Formica Corporation's global presence as the decór layer — with classified ads in Mandarin, Spanish, French, and English. *Rainforest Kraft* had the bold red and black icons of animals, hearts, and stars drawn by the children arranged over printed kraft paper. *Rainforest for Rent* combined the shapes with the newsprint. The Ellipse Eclipse Series had four variations based on a birch wood grain. *Ellipse Eclipse* featured ellipses rotating and sometimes overlapping above a background of Natural or Cherry stained wood, a tongue-in-cheek reference to the football-shaped patches used to repair plywood and a common symbol in Spear's work. The *Birch* wood grain was also available without overlays in Natural and Cherry colors for a more traditional pattern. Inspired by the appearance of agricultural fields as seen from an airplane, *Aerial Fields* was "a crazy quilt... a natural look hardened with industrialism." Spear used CAD software to create the designs and then printed, cut, and pasted to create the collage pattern which was available in Red, Kraft, and White. Finally, the Millennium Series included *Cosmos* which was composed of literal constellations and planets in reflective gold and silver on a black backdrop. Referencing the fenestration pattern of some of Spear's residential designs at the time, *Millennium* was composed of small rectangles in varying sizes floating randomly on either a black or *Birch* wood grain background.[28]

Millenium, 1979

Red Aerial Fields, 1997

Rainforest Kraft, 1997

Rainforest for Rent, 1997

**FORMICA®**

7296-43
TIGERWOOD
ARTISAN FINISH

**FORMICA®**

3495-RD
MINERAL
TERRA
RADIANCE FINISH

**FORMICA®**

7231-58
FALLEN LEAVES
MATTE FINISH

Crayon series, 1996

Trained as an architect and joining the company in 1989, in-house designer, Renee Hytry Derrington developed the realistic stone look of *Colorado Slate* in 1994, along with four diverse patterns debuting in 1996. *Terra* was a sophisticated pattern inspired by fine-grained sands from locations around the world. *Leaves* had a more realistic and dimensional look of leaves on a forest floor than in previous iterations and *Crayon* was a playful pattern of overlapping scribbles in various directions. There were two versions of a pattern that Hytry Derrington created using the seven letters of the company's name rotated and floating in a matrix of shapes: *Positive Text* had dark letters over a light background and *Reverse Text* was the opposite.

Stone series, 1999

Several more patterns by Hytry Derrington were released in 1999. Continuing the tradition of fabric patterns started by *Linen* in 1937, *Weave* was a textural design of tightly woven fibers with dynamic variation for a more natural, worn look. *Tigerwood* was a stylized version of the exotic wood grain. With a pattern reminiscent of David Hockney's paintings of dappled sunlight over rippling water in a swimming pool, *Sea* had a dark blue background and *Spa* a light turquoise. As solid surface countertops were becoming increasingly popular in the late 1990s, Hytry Derrington designed the Envision Series to create the look of solid surface in a laminate. The line has since been expanded multiple times. The Stone Series included four rough finishes and mottled patterns: grey *Concrete Stone*, red *Cotta Stone*, white *Lime Stone*, and beige *Sand Stone*.

*"How is a pattern first put down on paper? After analysis of the area to be considered (mainly vertical or horizontal, large or small, busy or plain, and the direction the design is to take) it may be started with pencil, paint, or actual material, as in the case of linen or wood. Or it may start with material and end as paint as the thinking on it changes. Sometimes the idea shifts from a rough pencil sketch to the thought it would be best in a photostat of an actual substance such as cracked china or peanuts. Very rarely does "drawing" accomplish the full range of a program alone. After completion of the comprehensive sketch, which may be painted or photographic, or hand-colored generic material, it is submitted for approval. Suggestions may modify the pattern, emphasize certain characteristics of it or strip it down to its basic concept for reworking. On the other hand, acceptance of it can be so spontaneous that there is no doubt of its ultimate success. Critics at all times keep in mind that the good design keeps the user happy, the aesthete unoffended, and the manufacturer 'in the black.'"*[29]

—*Jack Alexander*

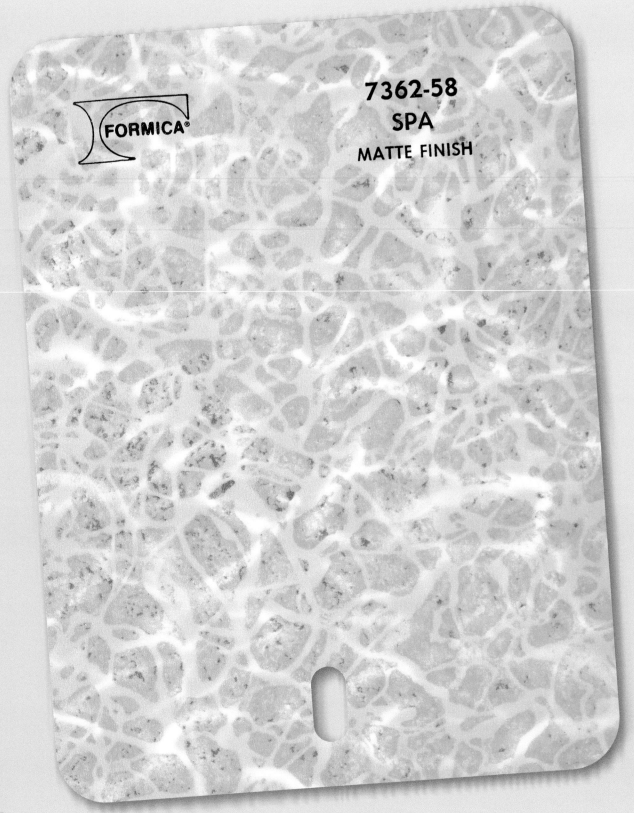

7362-58
SPA
MATTE FINISH

FORMICA®

American Granite series, 1986
Formica Patterns brochure, 1989

99

# CHAPTER FIVE

# 2000s & 2010s

The new millennium brought about the maturity of the age of globalization and information technology. The Internet, an expansion of international trade, and a shared global focus on combating climate change and terrorism all made the world feel more interconnected than ever. By 2000, mobile phones were widely adopted and the iPhone was introduced in 2007. The combination of constant access to the internet and widespread dissemination of powerful, pocket-sized computers fueled the rapid rise of social media, reality TV, and 24-hour news. During the first two decades of the 21st century, people also began

Glass series, 2001

Glaze series, 2001

focusing more attention on their homes as a way to create some controlled and quiet space in an ever-noisier and public world.

A resurgence of technicolored hues in graphic design became a key marketing element to grab attention in the endless stream of content from an increasingly decentralized group of creators. As a result, colors began to swing back toward the bright, vibrant hues of the 80s while the neutrals and soft hues of the 90s remained popular, especially in the home. In parallel, the popularity of home renovation programming on television and online communities devoted to sharing images of interior design amplified a trend toward monochromatic decorating. Black and white with endless shades of grey and greige populated commercial and residential interiors and stainless steel continued to be the most popular finish for appliances during this period.

# TIMELESS MATERIALS

By the beginning of the 21st century, Formica Group's lead designer Renee Hytry Derrington, working with an international team, directed many of the patterns for the company. As the popularity of granite countertops in the U.S. was rising dramatically at the time, Hytry Derrington created the *Butterum Granite* pattern in 2001. It was the most realistic granite look at the time in a laminate, created by scanning a tile of Giallo Veneziano stone. The same year, the company released various new pattern series. Designed to "represent transparency and retro influences," the *Glass* Series featured a crackle glass design. The *Paint* Series had an expressive pattern, inspired by linoleum which was making a comeback. Other lines focused on "naturalized textures using artistic hand-rendered techniques." The *Glaze* Series and *Ceramic* Series both had an antique crazed finish, that of *Ceramic* being more subtle. Meanwhile, the *Paper* Series had the appearance of traditional handmade paper. The colors of that year's patterns were organized into Warm and Cool Palettes, illustrating the general move away from the more saturated hues of the 90s. "Organic natural textures, honest materials, and whimsical trend looks [were] celebrated" in the 2001 Formica® laminate collection.[30]

Butterum Granite, Cotton Paper series, Paint series, 2001

Dogbone Storm, 2010

104

# OPTICAL SOLIDS

As the popularity of solid colors was diminishing, the Formica Group designers developed new optical solids, patterns that appear solid at a distance but have a fine grain and/or texture when viewed up close. In 2001, two new usable textured optical solids were introduced and the fine-grained sand *Terra* Series, previously released in 1996, was also restyled for that year's collection. The *Gauze* Series highlighted the qualities of the sheer fabric and the *.net* Series referenced the internet age with its delicate matrix. Next, the *Solidz*™ line debuted in 2002, designed to imitate the subtle fibers of MDF and stained in eight colors ranging from the neutrals of MDF and Cardboard to bright primaries like Blue and Red. Designed with the commercial sector in mind, the visual texture of *Solidz* helped hide wear and tear in high-traffic areas and the line's pattern referenced the trend in recycled looks and was marketed as "Solids with a Zing!" In 2010, a supplier provided a computer-generated, geometric pattern called *Dogbone* that served as the "new generation of optical solids." That same year, Formica Group in-house designer Gerri Chmiel designed two textile-inspired optical solids. *Weft* was soft and subtle in its woven appearance while *Warp* had a stronger, more graphic depiction of fabric. The *Duotex Series* of optical solids based on soft woven fabric textures was released in 2015.[31]

Cardboard Solidz, 2002

String.Net, 2001

Terra series, 1996

7710-58
COPPER
GAUZE
MATTE FINISH

# TEXTURAL THEMES

With the broad adoption of stainless steel for appliances and other surfaces during the late 90s and early 2000s, Formica Group designers developed a unique process to bring the look and feel of metal to plastic laminate. This gave designers the ability to achieve the realistic appearance and reflectivity of metal in a more durable and affordable material. The Authentix Collection was released in 2003 and included twelve combinations of pearlescent metallic colors (Copper, Aluminum, Stainless, and Brass) in various textures, ranging from subtle to highly dimensional. The collection featured the understated *Powdered*, the linear grain of *Brushed*, the raised squares of *Punched*, and the bas-relief diamonds of *Quilted*.

Released the same year, the Etchings™ Collection and Honed Collection were textured versions of the popular stone patterns, making Formica laminate even more competitive with granite. Another major source of competition during this period was engineered stone so at the same time Formica Group released *Crystall* and *Quartzite* to provide the appearance of quartz in a laminate. *MicroDot*™, released in 2005, advanced the texture-as-pattern concept with its subtle grid of tactile dots. It was available in a variety of colors including brights like Neon Yellow, Lime, Grenadine, and Cassis.[32]

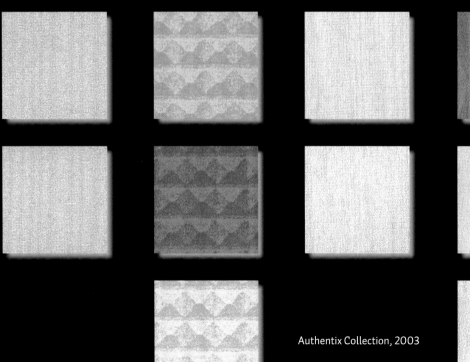

Authentix Collection, 2003

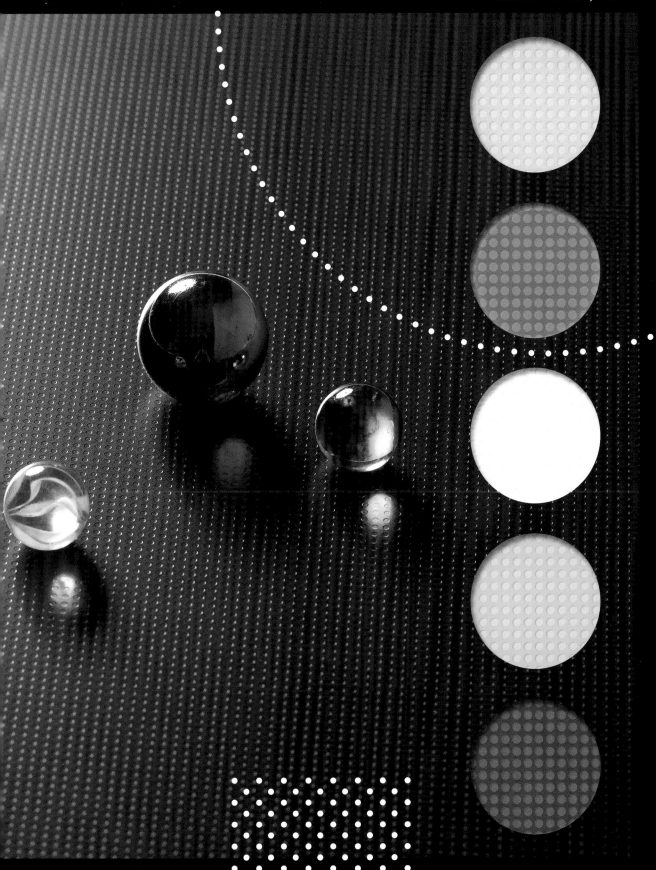

Beluga series, 2004

Strand series, 2007

Screen series, 2004

# ASIAN INFLUENCES

A trend toward Asian references occurred in the early 2000s. The *Mat* Series, released in 2003, was a woven pattern referencing the traditional floor coverings of some Asian countries and included blue Batik, yellow Sisal, and brown Tatami. Also debuting that year was the *Cane* Series, initially available only in the natural color of Bamboo as the fast-growing and sustainable plant was becoming a popular material for flooring and home goods around the world. The following year, Rattan was added which was a darker brown shade.

The *Screen* series was released in 2004 and looked "like aged industrial mesh, yet sheer and delicate." It was available in three colors: dark grey Painted, brown Shoji, and light grey Silk. Coming out the same year, *Beluga* was an abstract and dense pattern of circles inspired by the futuristic graphics of Japanese Anime. The standard color was a mix of greys with light green with Beige as another option. Formica Group collaborated with the Osaka-based surface design firm Designers FREE on two designs: *Strand,* a linear pattern akin to a brushed surface, in 2007; and *Sculpted*™, a pattern created with raised texture in undulating horizontal lines, in 2008.[33]

# CLASSICS COLLECTION

Due to frequent requests from consumers for period-appropriate patterns and a trend toward nostalgia, Formica Group created the Classics Collection in 2005, rereleasing *Boomerang* and *VirrVarr.* Perstorp, the Swedish company that created *VirrVarr* in 1958, had been acquired by Formica Group in 2000 so including it alongside *Boomerang* (originally called *Skylark*) was a way to celebrate the creative merging of the two companies. *Boomerang* was restyled in four historic colors including Aqua, Coral, Charcoal, and the original blue renamed Skylark as an homage. *VirrVarr*, which means criss-cross in Swedish, was designed by

Mat series, 2003

**6910-58**
**ELECTRIC**
**PLASTIQUE**
**MATTE FINISH**

**6909-58**
**GLASS**
**PLASTIQUE**
**MATTE FINISH**

Plastique series, 2005

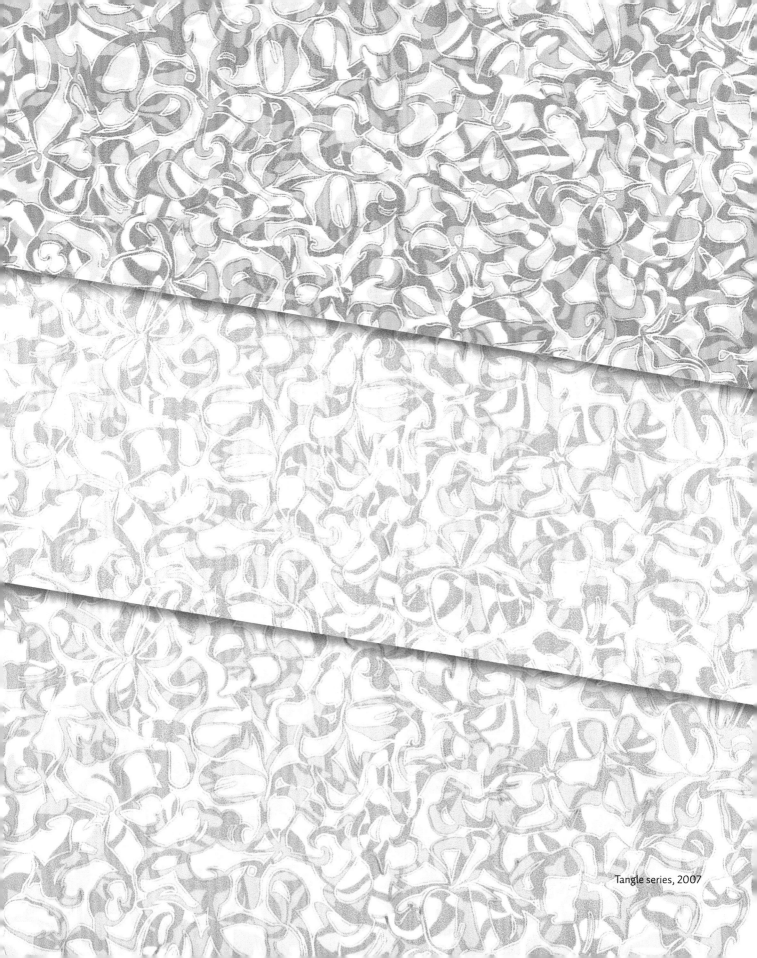

Tangle series, 2007

the Prince of Sweden in 1958 and was popular throughout the 1960s in Europe. Including *VirrVarr* in the Classics Collection made it the first time the pattern was available to purchase in North America and it came in the original colors of White and Light Blue. Designer Count Sigvard Bernadotte said, "it's a pattern — other than its name — that's smooth and vivid at the same time — lively enough to be applied on larger surfaces."[34]

Other patterns released in 2005 were *Plastique, Atomic, Metal,* and a new version of *Spa.* In 2007, the international in-house design team created the Tangle Series and Strand Series in a selection of muted browns, greens, and greys. *Tangle* used intertwining lines and freestyle images with positive and negative space to create a complex, graphic pattern. *Strand* used straight overlapping lines implying light and movement to form a linear pattern.

The Crete Series and Rust Series were introduced in 2006, adding to the library of patterns inspired by the industrial aesthetic. The Mineral Series, inspired by geology and crystalline structures, was released in 2008 and the six colors were named after actual minerals including yellow Ochre, golden Sepia, green Olivine, red Sienna, brown Umber, and dark Jet. *Travertine* had been introduced in 2004 and was expanded in 2008 after being ranked No. 1 for usable patterns in the company's residential survey that year.

# CONTEMPORARY ART

The Formica Corporation partnered with the Contemporary Arts Center (CAC) of Cincinnati in 2008 on FORM: Contemporary Architects at Play, an exhibition of new works by ten world-renowned designers including Peter Eisenman, Michael Graves, Zaha Hadid, Thom Mayne, Bill Pedersen, Laurinda Spear, Bernard Tschumi, Jaime Velez, Massimo Vignelli, and Buzz Yudell. The sculptural pieces were all created using Formica® decorative laminate and were auctioned off to raise funds for the museum's educational programming. The exhibition was revived and expanded at the CAC in 2013 as part of the Formica brand laminate's centennial celebration organized by Abbott Miller of Pentagram. In 2017, Formica Group and the CAC partnered on the FORM Student Innovation Competition, an annual program initially open to college students in the United

Metal series, 2008
Crete series, 2006

States and later to those in Canada and Mexico. Students must use three or more Formica brand products in their rendered entries, competing for cash prizes and the chance to have their design fabricated and displayed at NeoCon, one of the world's largest design expos.

# 180FX® SERIES

FORM: Contemporary Architects at Play exhibition, work by Peter Eisenman, 2008

The groundbreaking 180fx Series was developed in the mid-2000s, creating continuous visuals as large as five feet wide and in realistic color, using high-resolution flatbed scanning and a four-color printing process. This was the first time that technology allowed decorative laminate to have such expansive sheets of a non-repeating pattern and the advance happened as design trends continued to move toward open plans with the kitchen island as the centerpiece. After the Great Recession began in 2008, the project was stalled until Formica Group formed a Residential Industry Expert Roundtable in the late 2000s to test the concept of "large-scale and exotic" designs for residential applications. The focus group was comprised of the top designers from retailers, manufacturers, builders, and published trend experts including The Home Depot, Kraftmaid, and Sherwin Williams. They concluded, "if the design fits on a chip, it is no longer innovative," spurring the Formica Group design staff to move forward with production and release of the 180fx line.

The first patterns were based on granite which was still the most popular stone for residential kitchen counters at that time. Renee Hytry Derrington traveled to the quarries of South America and the Mediterranean to search for the perfect specimens for the new line. One of the nine releases that year was *Blue Storm Granite*, using a slab of rare blue granite from Brazil. Others included the Mascarello Series, the Yellow River Series, the Red Montana Series, and Espirito Santo. As marble countertops were overtaking granite in popularity, the company introduced the

Sequoia series, 180fx® Collection

Crema Mascarello, 2012

Antique Mascarello, 2009

Yellow River, 2009

Blue Storm, 2009

Petrified Wood, 2010

Red Montana, 2009

Espírito Santo, 2009

Calacatta Marble, 2011

Soapstone Sequoia, 2010

richly-detailed *Calacatta Marble* in 2011. Based on one of the world's most rare and sought-after stones, it was the first full-scale realistic representation of marble in laminate without a repeating pattern across the width of the laminate sheet. Other 180fx patterns released that year included the warm stones of *Breccia Paradiso, Travertine Silver, Soapstone Sequoia, Slate Sequoia, Black Fossilstone,* and the stunning colors of *Petrified Wood*. Now sold by all Formica Group global divisions, the 180fx line has continued to expand and remains one of the company's most popular laminate ranges.[35]

# GRAPHIC PATTERNS

Based on a small-scale graphic by professional surface designer Tracy Reinberg, *Geo* was released in 2010. Inspired by the view of networks on Earth as seen from the upper atmosphere, *Geo* was a tangle of lines "orderly and chaotic at the same time." Patterns released in 2013 included *Drops* which was a "graphic yet organic, through the play of imperfect dots on horizontal lines" and *Twill* with its play on the traditional fabric, adding a diagonal grid to the woven pattern. The Hex Series, "a pattern gradation, modernized with the hexagon shape," was introduced in 2015 with two color options — gray Folkstone and dark gray Storm.[36]

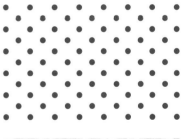

Drops series, 2013

Twill series, 2013

Geo series, 2010

Hex series, 2015

# ANNIVERSARY COLLECTION

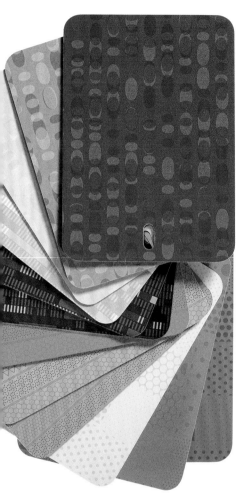

To mark its centennial in 2013, Formica Group hired the design firm Pentagram to create the Anniversary Collection of patterns; a refresh of the brand logo; anniversary gifts; and an exhibit and book, both titled *Formica Forever*. Pentagram, the world's largest independent design consultancy, is known for its innovative work in a wide range of fields including environmental, graphic, corporate, industrial, and interior design. Designed by Pentagram's Abbott Miller with Renee Hytry Derrington, the collection included four new patterns. *Ellipse* was composed of rows of varying light and dark ellipses — using the "hidden oval" found in the Formica brand logo — overlapping to create a rhythm. *Endless* used light and dark bars in thin rows to create the effect of a computer's processor in motion. The pointillist art of *Dotscreen* featured "luminous colors with extremely fine micro-dots in continuous ribbons." *Halftone* used "near-bright colors patterned with various sizes of toned dots, reminiscent of halftone printing screens." *Ellipse* and *Endless* used a similar printing method as the Kaleidoscopic technique used in the 1950s for *Milano*. By making the rotogravure cylinder different circumferences, it ensured that no two printed sheets would be identical and created "seemingly infinite patterns that appear consistent due to the fluidity of the overlapping elements." Each of the Anniversary Collection patterns integrated the Formica® logo as a subtle, tone-on-tone watermark.

> "Developing this iconic brand's 100th Anniversary Collection was inspiring. Formica laminate is extraordinary because of its Zelig-like nature, blurring the past, present and future while completely crossing all social and economic categories. It's a material with distinctive tactility, a warmth and domesticity; it's man-made, yet has attained a natural quality in our lives. The heart and soul of Formica laminate is a printed sheet. Pattern and color are intrinsic to the culture of the company, so exploring the translucency of ink and the interaction of pattern and color was a natural area for me."
>
> — Abbott Miller[37]

Halftone series, 2013

Endless series, 2013

Ellipse series, 2013

Dotscreen series, 2013

117

Flow series, 2014

# EARTH MATERIALS

Referred to as a "chameleon" for its versatility, the Elemental Series featured a large-scale pattern that could be interpreted as concrete, metal, and stone. *Elemental Concrete* was designed to appear like weathered cement and is still one of the top-three selling patterns ten years later. The Flow Series and the Paloma Series were created in 2014 as part of a shift to appeal to the Millennial consumer. *Flow* was based on the fine grains of linear sandstone and *Paloma*'s pattern was similar to quartzite. *Formwood* was designed by Renee Hytry Derrington in 2015 to expand the options for concrete. Based on the incidental patterns created in concrete by construction boards, *Formwood* was developed using input from a focus group. Concrete was poured onto reclaimed barn wood, cured, and then stained — with the end result scanned for production. *Star Dune*, released in 2017, was comprised of "chocolate brown veins swirling around caramel colored pieces of matrix" and was seen as an alternative for consumers fatigued with granite. *Layered Sand* was made by layering various scales and colors of sand into a frame and compacting each layer, similar to rammed earth architecture. The frames were then laid horizontal and scanned to use their unique linear patterns. Created in 2019, it was a subtle pattern with an appropriately sandy texture, available in three colorways: White, Black, and the hues of natural sand.

Elemental series, 2013

Black Layered Sand, 2019

Formwood series, 2015

The Formica Group began collaborating with the potter, designer, and entrepreneur Jonathan Adler in 2014. Adler designed three patterns in his signature bold and colorful style released in January 2015. *Malachite* used the distinct pattern created by cutting the eponymous mineral, though rather than the greens of natural malachite, this pattern was offered in the unexpected colors of bright Blue, vibrant Orange, and moody Charcoal. *Greek Key* was a tone-on-tone diagonal pattern based on the ancient design — a common motif in Adler's work — and available in the same palette as *Malachite*. Taking inspiration from his love of mid-century modern upholstery, *Lacquered Linen* echoed one of the oldest Formica laminate patterns and was available in Orange and Charcoal as well as a happy Green and classic Crème. In August 2015, the collection expanded to include White versions of *Malachite* and *Greek Key* along with *Splatter* — white paint splattered with "carefree precision" over Navy and Gray. In January 2016, two additional patterns were released: *Grasscloth* and *Josef Linen*. The former was inspired by one of Adler's favorite wallpapers, real grass cloth, while the latter is an homage to Josef Albers, the mid-20th century artist and theorist who taught at the Bauhaus, Black Mountain College, and Yale.[38]

Malachite series, 2015
Laquered Linen series, 2015
Navy Splatter, 2016

# LAMINATE AS MARKERBOARD

As the trend for chalkboard paint and customizable wall coverings took off, Formica Group introduced the Writable Surfaces Collection, providing "a cheery writing surface for message centers, menu boards, grocery lists, and calendar notes." The collection began in 2017 with *LoveWords*, a tag cloud-style pattern of words related to affection and family. *HappyWords* was introduced a year later and featured a textual pattern of words related to contentment in English, Spanish, and French, in bright but transparent colors. Later additions in the collection included the fanciful flowers of *ColorBook*, designed in-house by Kathleen Streitenberger and inspired by coloring books designed for all ages; *ImageGrid*™, a graph paper pattern created by a partner printer and styled by Renee Hytry Derrington; and *ChalkAble*® which had the classic look of a chalkboard and was available in Black and Gray.

LoveWords, ColorBook
and ImagiGrid, 2017

# ECO DECÓR SERIES

Renee Hytry Derrington was renovating her home's basement in 2014 and decided to use a more sustainable insulation product made of shredded denim from discarded jeans. The material inspired her to see if, rather than scan denim and print the image on paper as would normally be done for a laminate, she could use the material itself as the patterned top layer. This led to *Reclaimed Denim Fiber* which was created using reclaimed post-industrial material from clothing mills instead of paper. Every sheet of Formica laminate was unique since it was made of actual cotton and no dyes were added so the colors of the fabric varied as well. Released in 2015, it was the first in the Eco Decór Series. Reclaimed Denim Fiber won a Red Dot Design Award in 2017, the jury calling it, "an unusual as well as environmentally-friendly use of material."

Two years later, another novel laminate product was created, this time using reclaimed paper. Using scraps left over during the production of solid-colored paper, the designers at Formica Group developed a process for small-batch production of one-of-a-kind sheets of decór paper that emulated terrazzo flooring. *Paper Terrazzo* further highlighted its materiality with a unique finish with a paper feel, allowing the slightly raised pieces to create tactile interest. Paper Terrazzo was named Best of the Year in the Green Innovation Category by Interior Design Magazine.

The final entry in the series was introduced in 2019 and was perhaps the most meta of the Formica laminates to date. Using 100% recycled and reclaimed materials, the decorative layer was designed to highlight the humble kraft paper that has been hidden within Formica® laminate all these years. Hytry Derrington and the design staff used a combination of pre- and post-consumer recycled paper along with reclaimed materials such as chaff from coffee beans, burlap from coffee bags, and peat moss to create *Recycled Kraft* and its authentic look and feel. Again, no two pieces of laminate were identical since each decór sheet was made individually and it was the first decorative laminate to be certified 100% recycled content by the Forest Stewardship Council (FSC).[39]

Paper Terrazzo series, 2017

Reclaimed Denim Fiber, 2015

Felt series, 2019

Green Felt, 2019

# SOFTNESS AND SUBTLY

In 2017, in-house designers worked with a supplier's design staff to create a unique and beautiful pattern using a shallow bath of water, oil, paint, and soap for the Bubble Series. The delicate design was created by carefully lowering the decór paper onto the bath, leaving a totally random popping effect on the paper. The Paint Scrape Series, also released in 2017, was created in-house after Formica Group designer Scott Dannenfelser was inspired by a show at the Tate Modern. Layer upon layer of paint was applied and then scraped off in a cross-grid pattern. In 2019, the company released *Felt* which had both the soft look and familiar tactile feel of the woolen fabric.

Paint Scrape series, 2017

Bubble series, 2017

125

# CLOSING

# 2020s

# & BEYOND

**T**he beginning years of the 2020s were largely characterized by a historic global pandemic, skyrocketing inflation, and social and political upheaval around the world. This chaotic and often stressful period has led people to focus even more intensely on creating safe and comforting interior spaces at home and elsewhere. An increased focus on environmental and social issues among institutions, corporations, and the public has pushed the design community to analyze processes and sourcing and to explore more sustainable methods of production. This includes seeking ways to make products that support human health and wellness by eliminating harmful chemicals and by bringing biophilic design and natural patterns and colors to interiors.

In-house Formica Group designers and a partner rotogravure printer created three patterns using hand-painted artwork at a large scale that could utilize the capabilities unlocked with the 180fx Series. Though each was unique, the patterns were inspired by marble and used paint as the primary medium. Influenced by the sense of movement in the veining of natural stone, *Painted Marble* was created by trying to mix water-based paints and oils. This hydrophobic interaction was used by the decór printer in 2020 to create an elegant, flowing pattern in neutral colors. Formica Group design coordinator Kathleen "Fred" Streitenberger was a professional artist by training and the company partnered with her on two original patterns created using hand painting techniques. Initially starting out as a side project, she utilized a blow dryer and compressed air to manipulate gouache paints and alcohol on large sheets of wet paper to create the evocative and translucent patterns of *Watercolor* in 2020. Two years later, Streitenberger designed another entry in the 180fx line, reviving one of Formica Group's earliest experimentations with pattern: marbled paper. Paint was artfully dripped over a canvas and then worked to create the flowing swirls of *Marbled Gray*.[40]

Painted Marble series, 2020

Watercolor series, 2020

Marbled Gray, 2022

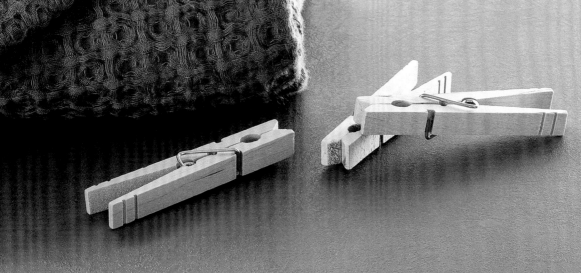

The most recent patterns released by the company in 2022 have continued the traditions of innovation, handcrafting, and tying the patterns to nature. *Monolith* represented the next generation of using texture and finish to imbue patterns on solid colors. Designed in-house by Eva Hoernisch and Renee Hytry Derrington, *Monolith*'s large swirls of varying textures and sheens are reminiscent of cut stone. The low sheen, tone-on-tone finish, and non-repeating pattern contribute to the natural slate look and feel. Formica Group designer Gerri Chmiel developed a versatile pattern resembling the natural patina found on stone, concrete, or metal. The *Patine* Series was available in the mottled grey of Concrete and in the coppery tones of Bronze.

Hytry Derrington further expanded the arboreal inventory of Formica® decorative laminate with more patterns. *Birchbark* was created by scanning pieces of the white bark and curating the images to create the comforting familiarity of birch trees as a laminate surface. The *Brushstroke* Series, though representing the linear nature of paint strokes on a surface, was seen as an abstraction of woodgrain. The Brushstroke Series was available in three colors: the off-white Pale, the light brown of Wood, and the terra cotta Earthenware. Created with hand-crumpled paper, the shadows and texture of *Paperfold* leaned on the yearning for nostalgia. The *Cloth* Series continued the evolution of *Linen* with a sophisticated and subtle herringbone pattern. Designed as a "broken twill," the Cloth Series was available in crisp white Cotton, warm khaki Woolen, and cool aqua Glass.

Woodland Marble, 2022

132

Birchbark, 2022

Inspired by the work of Brokisglass, a Czech start-up that worked with a lighting manufacturer and glass artists to fuse chips of reclaimed glass into usable materials, Gerri Chmiel wanted to create the look of glass in a laminate surface. Using chips of reclaimed glass in a bath of milk and sugar, *Sugar Glass* was designed to appear as if "translucent blue-gray glass was floating weightlessly within a sheet of opaque white glass." In a nod to one of the company's earliest patterns, the opalescent and ephemeral character of *Sugar Glass* can be seen as a descendant of *Decorated* (1937) and *Pearl* (1949).[41]

2023 marks the 110th anniversary of the Formica Group. Today, Formica laminate designers and their partners are continuing the traditions established by the company's founders in the early decades of technical and artistic innovation in decorative laminate patterns. Just as those engineers and printers pushed the boundaries on the capabilities of sheet laminate and experimented with ways to create patterns and colors, today's designers and technicians are exploring new ways to update Formica brand laminate into the future.

Sugar Glass, 2022

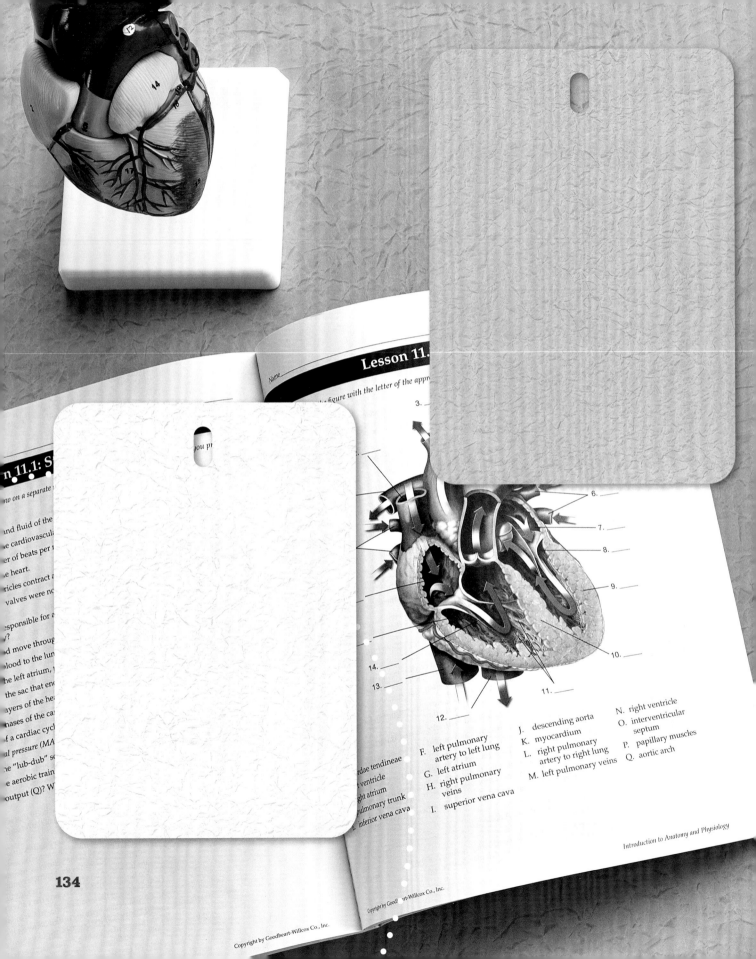

## Lesson 11.

_...a figure with the letter of the appro..._

3. _____

6. _____

7. _____

8. _____

9. _____

10. _____

11. _____

12. _____

13. _____

14. _____

n 11.1: S

_ow on a separate_

_...nd fluid of the_
_...e cardiovascula_
_...er of beats per_
_...e heart._
_...ricles contract_
_...valves were n_

_...esponsible for_
_...?_
_...d move throug_
_...lood to the lun_
_...he left atrium,_
_...the sac that en_
_...ayers of the he_
_...nases of the ca_
_...f a cardiac cycl_
_...al pressure (MA_
_...he "lub-dub" s_
_...e aerobic train_
_...output (Q)? W_

_...rdae tendineae_
_...t ventricle_
_...ght atrium_
_...pulmonary trunk_
_... inferior vena cava_

F. left pulmonary
    artery to left lung
G. left atrium
H. right pulmonary
    veins
I. superior vena cava

J. descending aorta
K. myocardium
L. right pulmonary
    artery to right lung
M. left pulmonary veins

N. right ventricle
O. interventricular
    septum
P. papillary muscles
Q. aortic arch

Introduction to Anatomy and Physiology

134

Paperfold series, 2022

The narrative thread of Formica laminate patterns can be said to traverse the realms of science, technology, handcraft, artistry, storytelling, and nature. From the trees that become the paper and the ancient organisms that become the plastics to the minerals that are used for the inks and the metals that create the cylinders and press plates, Formica laminate is tied to the Earth. So it is appropriate that so many of the patterns and themes over its history have also taken cues from the planet and our cosmos. From the early experiments with natural and artistic patterns to the hand-drawn graphics of Boomerang (Skylark) and the more recent explorations using technology to print realistic material images, Formica decorative laminate is in a constant cycle of iteration, revival, innovation, and reinvention.

Perhaps the next chapter in the story of Formica decorative laminate will not only bring us new and exciting patterns, but also new ways to make the material even more sustainable. Imagine a laminate made with paper that is 100% recycled or sustainably harvested from rapidly-growing plants, plastics created from renewable or bio-based materials, and factories and shipping powered exclusively by solar and wind power.

Just as in 1913, the company continues to meld technological ingenuity and thoughtful design to evolve its signature engineered material and deliver a supremely adaptable product that responds to the challenges of its time. It is through that evolution that a simple material from the turn of the last century can not only join in the latest threads of conversation around sustainability and design but help push the design discourse forward. ∎

Sugar Glass, 2022

# BIBLIOGRAPHY

Adamson, Glenn. *Industrial Strength Design: How Brooks Stevens Shaped Your World*. Milwaukee, WI: Milwaukee Art Museum, 2003.

Alexander, Jack. "Patterns: And How They Got That Way." *This Formica World* vol. 10 no. 4. (October 1959): 2-3.

*Architectural Forum*. (Article on Sanders' townhome). March 1936: 157.

*Architectural Forum*. "Plastics in Architecture." February 1937: 147-150.

*Architectural Forum*. "City House, New York, New York, Morris B. Sanders, Architect." August 1937: 87-88.

Baum, Arthur W. "The World Goes Plastic." *Saturday Evening Post*, vol. 222 issue 47 (May 20, 1950).

Bradbury, Dominic. *Mid-Century Modern Design: A Complete Sourcebook*. New York: Thames & Hudson, 2020.

*British Plastics and Moulded Products Trader*. "U.S.A. Plastics Contest: Modern Plastics Awards." November 1936: 272-273.

Brooks Stevens Archive. Milwaukee Art Museum, Milwaukee, WI.

Casey, Andrew. *Lucienne Day: In the Spirit of the Age*. Woodbridge, Suffolk, UK: Antique Collectors' Club, 2014.

Chase, Herbert. "Laminated Plastics Make Rapid Advances in USA." *British Plastics and Moulded Products Trader*. November 1936: 277-280.

de Leon, Sharon. Interviews by Renee Hytry Derrington. August - September 2022.

Fehrman, Cherie and Kenneth Fehrman. *Postwar Interior Design: 1945-1960*. New York: Van Nostrand Reinhold Company, 1987.

Ford, Robert. Interviews by Renee Hytry Derrington. August - October 2022.

Formica Corporate Archive, 1913-2023. Formica Group, Cincinnati, OH.

Formica Corporation. *Formica Forever*. Cincinnati, OH: Formica Corp. in assoc. with Metropolis Books, 2013.

Formica Corporation. *The World's Fair House: American Contemporary Styling at its Best*. Cincinnati, OH: Formica Corp, 1964.

Heller, Steven. "Tibor Kalman, 'Bad Boy' of Graphic Design, 49, Dies." *New York Times*, May 5, 1999.

Holusha, John. "Brooks Stevens, 83, Giant in Industrial Design." *New York Times*, January 7, 1995.

*Interiors*. "Morris Sanders obituary." October 1948.

Jackson, Lesley. *Robin and Lucienne Day: Pioneers of Modern Design*. New York: Princeton Architectural Press, 2001.

Lausch, William. Interview by Renee Hytry Derrington. July 2022.

Lewin, Susan Grant, ed. *Formica & Design: From the Counter Top to High Art*. New York: Rizzoli International Publications, 1991.

Marra, Diana. Interviews by Renee Hytry Derrington. July - October 2022.

McCann, Hiram. *Formica: Forty Years of Steady Vision*. Cincinnati, OH: Formica Co., 1953.

*Modern Plastics*. "What's New in Decorative Laminates." Vol. 28 (October 1950): 73-74.

National Museum of American History Archives Center, Formica Materials.

*Progressive Architecture*. "High Impact Material." August 1979: 89-93.

Raymond Loewy Archive, 1903-1982. Hagley Museum and Library, Wilmington, DE.

Reilly, Paul. "A Decorative Future for Plastics Laminates." *Design* vol. 6 issue 72 (December 1954): 9-13.

Roberts, Sam. "Jeremiah Goodman, Portraitist of Gilded Homes, Dies at 94." *New York Times*, September 12, 2017.

Sanders, Morris. 1950. Sheet of Decorative Material or the Like. U.S. Patent 157,633, filed August 24, 1948, and issued March 7, 1950.

Shaw, Marybeth. Interview by Renee Hytry Derrington. September 2022.

*This Formica World*. "Moonglo - New Formica Pattern." October 1948: 3-4.

Tubb, Shawn Patrick. *Cincinnati's Terrace Plaza Hotel: An Icon of American Modernism*. Cincinnati: Cincinnati Book Publishing, 2013.

Walker, Anthony. "Plastics: The Building Blocks of the Twentieth Century." *Construction History* vol. 10 (1994): 67-88.

Wright, Mary and Russel Wright. *Guide to Easier Living*. New York: Simon and Schuster, 1950.

# NOTES

1. Marybeth Shaw, "Evolutions in Surface Design," *Formica & Design: From the Counter Top to High Art* (New York: Rizzoli, 1991), 60-63.

2. Hiram McCann, *Formica: Forty Years of Steady Vision* (Cincinnati: Formica Co., 1953).

3. Hiram McCann, *Formica: Forty Years of Steady Vision* (Cincinnati: Formica Co., 1953).

4. Marybeth Shaw, "Evolutions in Surface Design," in *Formica & Design: From the Counter Top to High Art*, ed. Susan Grant Lewin (New York: Rizzoli, 1991), 45-47.

5. Jeffrey L. Meikle, "Plastics," in *Formica & Design: From the Counter Top to High Art*, ed. Susan Grant Lewin (New York: Rizzoli, 1991), 45-47.

6. Jack Alexander, "Patterns and How They Got That Way," *This Formica World* (Cincinnati: Formica Co., 1959).

7. Hiram McCann, *Formica: Forty Years of Steady Vision* (Cincinnati: Formica Co., 1953).

8. Shawn Patrick Tubb, Cincinnati's Terrace Plaza Hotel: An Icon of American Modernism (Cincinnati: Cincinnati Book Publishing, 2013).

9. "Morris Sanders Obituary," *Interiors* (October 1948).

10. "Moonglo - New Formica Pattern," *This Formica World* (Cincinnati: Formica Co., October 1948).

11. Marybeth Shaw, "Evolutions in Surface Design," *Formica & Design: From the Counter Top to High Art* (New York: Rizzoli, 1991), 64-65.

12. Glenn Adamson, Industrial Strength Design: How Brooks Stevens Shaped Your World (Cambridge, MA: The MIT Press, 2003).

13. Jack Alexander, "Patterns and How They Got That Way," *This Formica World* (Cincinnati: Formica Co., 1959).

14. Casey, Andrew, *Lucienne Day: In the Spirit of the Age*, (Woodbridge, Suffolk, UK: Antique Collectors' Club, 2014) 50-52.

15. Lesley Jackson, *Robin and Lucienne Day: Pioneers of Modern Design* (New York: Princeton Architectural Press, 2001).

16. Jeffrey L. Meikle, "Plastics," *Formica & Design: From the Counter Top to High Art* (New York: Rizzoli, 1991), 52.

17. Marybeth Shaw, "Evolutions in Surface Design," *Formica & Design: From the Counter Top to High Art* (New York: Rizzoli, 1991), 69 and interviews with Bob Ford and Sharon de Leon.

18. Steven Holt, "The Formica History: It Isn't What You Think," *Formica & Design: From the Counter Top to High Art* (New York: Rizzoli, 1991), 32.

19. Formica Group, corporate archive video The History of Formica Corporation, 1983.

20. Marybeth Shaw, "Evolutions in Surface Design," *Formica & Design: From the Counter Top to High Art* (New York: Rizzoli, 1991), 73-76.

21. Formica Group, corporate archive materials.

22. Marybeth Shaw, "Evolutions in Surface Design," in *Formica & Design: From the Counter Top to High Art*, ed. Susan Grant Lewin (New York: Rizzoli, 1991), 73-77.

23. "Design Pulse: The Venturi Collection," Knoll, Inc., accessed December 11, 2022, https://www.knoll.com/story/shop/robert-venturi-q-a.

24. Steven Holt "The Formica History: It Isn't What You Think," in *Formica & Design: From the Counter Top to High Art*, ed. Susan Grant Lewin (New York: Rizzoli, 1991), 36.

25. Jeffrey L. Meikle, "Plastics," in *Formica & Design: From the Counter Top to High Art*, ed. Susan Grant Lewin (New York: Rizzoli, 1991), 55-56.

26. Alessandro De Gregori, "The Autonomous Image," in *Formica & Design: From the Counter Top to High Art*, ed. Susan Grant Lewin (New York: Rizzoli, 1991), 78-79.

27. Formica Corporation, "Light and Illusion: Introducing the Refractions and Phantoms Collections," *Surface Level: The Complete Book of Laminate Surfaces from Formica Collection*, 1993.

28. Formica Corporation, *The Laurinda Spear Collection: New Laminate Designs from Formica Corporation*, 1998.

29. Jack Alexander, "Patterns and How They Got That Way," *This Formica World* (Cincinnati: Formica Co., 1959).

30. Formica Group, *Formica Brand Laminate: The Art of Being Modern* product catalog, 2001.

31. Formica Group, product catalogs 2001/2002, and other corporate archive materials.

32. Formica Group, *Authentix Collection 2003: The Art of Imitating Metal* and other product catalogs, 2003/2004/2005.

33. Formica Group, product catalogs, 2003/2004, and other corporate archive materials.

34. Formica Group, product catalog 2005, and other corporate archive materials.

35. Formica Group, corporate archive materials and staff interviews.

36. Formica Group, corporate archive materials.

37. Abbott Miller, Anniversary Collection press release, Formica Group, 2013.

38. Formica Group, corporate archive materials.

39. Formica Group, corporate archive materials and staff interviews.

40. Formica Group, corporate archive materials and website.

41. Formica Group, corporate archive materials and staff interviews.

## ABOUT THE AUTHOR

**SHAWN PATRICK TUBB** is a licensed architect, historian, and author with a passion for historic preservation, especially mid-century modern design. He serves on the boards of preservation-related organizations and has worked to save buildings throughout North America.

Shawn received dual Master's degrees in Architecture and Community Planning from the University of Cincinnati, where he focused on preservation and sustainability. His first book, the award-winning *Cincinnati's Terrace Plaza Hotel: An Icon of American Modernism*, explored the landmark hotel's history and impact, notably featuring Formica decorative laminate throughout its state-of-the-art rooms and public spaces.

Shawn developed an appreciation for the complexities and interconnectedness of global design through his work and education in Shanghai, Mexico City, Brussels, Toronto, New York, and Los Angeles. He currently lives in Cincinnati, Ohio with his partner and their two rescue dogs.

## IMAGE CREDITS

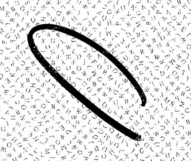

Positive Text, 1996